I did something that I don't recommend. When I received the manuscript for the devotional, See Jesus in the Pentateuch and Job. I read it in one session. To do it right it needs to be read over a ninety-day period and an opportunity to savor and pray about each one of the devotionals.

I've known Jim and Jacqie for over forty years. I had the privilege of being their pastor for approximately seven years in Farmington Minnesota. They are two of the finest Christian leaders I have had the privilege of knowing. They were people who were highly devoted to Jesus Christ in the church, they made a point of demonstrating it by their commitment to the word, to fellowship and acts of service. We've heard that we need to be fully devoted followers of Jesus Christ. Jim and Jacqie demonstrated what it truly meant to be devoted and a follower of Jesus Christ.

This devotional gleans rich nuggets from the Pentateuch, and also from the book of Job. I always love a fresh perspective on the word of God. This devotional is inspirational, practical yet challenging and convicting.

I encourage you to read it carefully and prayerfully.

—Jerry A Strandquist,
Retired but still looking for places to serve
(Pastor Strandquist was Senior Pastor at Cedar Valley Assembly of God in Bloomington, Minnesota, before his retirement.)

"Faith comes by hearing, and hearing by the Word of God." Being mentored in ministry as a teenager by Jacqie embedded this text into my Spirit. And it rang in my heart when Jacqie told me her theme of this devotional. She said, "Jesus is everywhere in the Old Testament." You are going to have an encounter with the Word revealed in a fresh way from the pages of the Old Testament as you journey through this devotional. Get ready to discover again or anew, "in the beginning was the Word!"

—MARK AND TERESA OLSON
PASTORS AT BLESSINGS.CHURCH
LITCHFIELD, MINNESOTA

Jacqie Kruger's new devotion book will be a blessing to you. The format is easy to follow, the material well worded, and the prayers heart felt. It will be equally enjoyed by those just beginning their journey of faith as well as those with years of study behind them. It's a stroll through Old Testament stories and lessons that believers should take. I recommend adding this to your continuing discipleship journey.

—DICK GRUBER, DMIN
CHILDREN'S PASTOR AT CROSSPOINT CHURCH
WAVERLY, IOWA

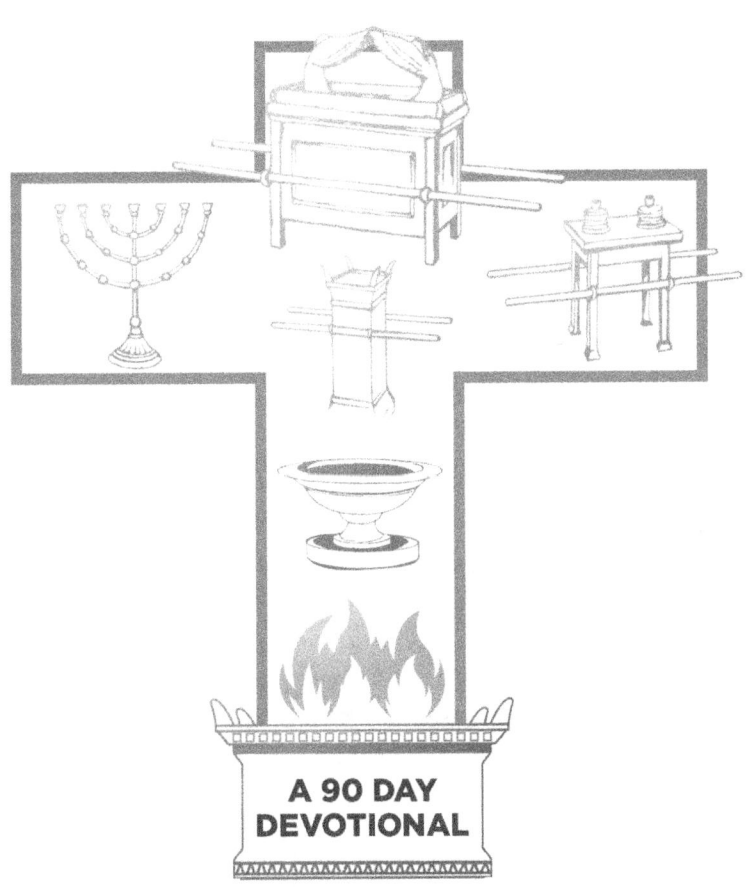

A 90 DAY DEVOTIONAL

SEE JESUS
IN THE
OLD TESTAMENT

SEE JESUS IN THE OLD TESTAMENT

THE PENTATEUCH AND JOB

A 90 DAY DEVOTIONAL

JACQUELYN KRUGER

See Jesus in the Old Testament (the Pentateuch and Job):
A 90-Day Devotional by Jacquelyn Kruger
Published by Manna and Miracles LLC
198 Gentle Drive, Almo, KY 42020

This book or parts thereof may not be reproduced in any form, stored in a retrieval system, or transmitted in any form by any means—electronic, mechanical, photocopy, recording, or otherwise—without prior written permission of the publisher, except as provided by United States of America copyright law.

Unless otherwise noted, all Scripture quotations are taken from the New Spirit Filled Life Bible, New King James Version, © 2002 by Thomas Nelson, Inc.

Scripture quotations marked KJV are from the King James Version of the Bible.

Scripture quotations marked NIV are taken from the Holy Bible, New International Version®, NIV®. Copyright © 1973, 1978, 1984, 2011 by Biblica, Inc.™ Used by permission of Zondervan. All rights reserved worldwide. www.zondervan.com. The "NIV" and "New International Version" are trademarks registered in the United States Patent and Trademark Office by Biblica, Inc.™

Scripture quotations marked NLT are from the Holy Bible, New Living Translation, copyright © 1996, 2004, 2007. Used by permission of Tyndale House Publishers, Inc., Wheaton, IL 60189. All rights reserved.

Scripture quotations marked TPT are from The Passion Translation®. Copyright © 2017, 2018, 2020 by Passion & Fire Ministries, Inc. Used by permission. All rights reserved. ThePassionTranslation.com.

Copyright © 2023 by Jacquelyn Kruger
All rights reserved

International Standard Book Number: 978-1-7352282-7-3
E-book ISBN: 978-1-7352282-8-0

While the author has made every effort to provide accurate internet addresses at the time of publication, neither the publisher nor the author assumes any responsibility for errors or for changes that occur after publication. Further, the publisher does not have any control over and does not assume any responsibility for author or third-party websites or their content.

23 24 25 26 27 28 — 987654321

Printed in the United States of America

*This book is lovingly dedicated to
Our three wonderful daughters:
Janine Kruger, Jennifer Revell, and
JoEllyn Leimola, who have always been
there to give unconditional love, prayer support, and practical suggestions and advice.*

Contents

Acknowledgments xv

Foreword xvii

Genesis 1–Genesis 22 1

Job 21

Genesis 23–Genesis 50 45

Exodus 69

Leviticus 105

Numbers 129

Deuteronomy 159

Notes 181

Acknowledgments

THANKS TO MY wonderful husband who has been my most faithful cheerleader and helper in this project. His prayers, wise advice and computer skills have been invaluable and without which this devotional would not have been written.

Thanks also to Jennifer Revell and Megan Revell for their excellent editing work.

Foreword

"Now there were some Greeks among those who went up to worship at the festival. They came to Philip, who was from Bethsaida in Galilee, with a request. "Sir," they said, "we would like to see Jesus." Philip went to tell Andrew; Andrew and Philip in turn told Jesus."
—JOHN 12:20–22

THE CRY OF every human heart should be to see Jesus. In her special ninety-day devotional, *See Jesus*, Jacqie Kruger helps the reader see or receive revelation of Jesus in the Book of Job and the Pentateuch. Your understanding of God will soar as you see how Old Testament narratives reveal so much about the character, nature, and purpose of our Lord. Your faith will grow, and you will be encouraged as you read each Word-filled devotion, discover practical insights for living, and pray the powerful prayers provided for each day.

—ART HEINZ, PHD
LEAD PASTOR, HOPE HARBOR CHURCH
MURRAY, KENTUCKY

Genesis 1–Genesis 22

DAY 1

IN THE BEGINNING

In the beginning God created the heavens and the earth.
—GENESIS 1:1; READ ALSO GENESIS 1

WE CAN SEE Jesus in the very first verse of the Bible. In Colossians 1:16 it is written, *"For by Him (Jesus) all things were created that are in heaven and that are on earth, visible and invisible, whether thrones or dominions or principalities or powers. All things were created through Him and for Him."* Jesus is clearly revealed here as creator.

We also see the trinity in the first three verses. We see Jesus as creator in verse one as explained in Colossians. In verse two and three the Bible says: *"The earth was without form, and void; and darkness was on the face of the deep. And the Spirit of God was hovering over the face of the waters. Then God said, 'Let there be light'; and there was light."* We are introduced to the role the Holy Spirit played in creation. He hovered over the face of the waters. Then God the Father spoke.

In verse 26 of chapter one it says: *"Then God said, 'Let US make man in Our image, according to Our likeness...'"* The reason the Bible uses the plural form is because the

Father, Son, and Holy Spirit were all involved in the very beginning of creation.

God goes on to say that He created man in His own image—*"male and female He created them."* The man and woman were a microcosm of the church, showing that God's glory would be seen in the combined expression of male and female. The record of redemption begins right here in the Garden of Eden where Adam and Eve were placed. Yes, the Gospel begins right here at the beginning of creation.

PRAYER

> *Thank You, Lord, for the miracle of creation. You created us in Your image and gave us dominion over the earth. As Your image bearers, we hold inestimable value and worth. We praise You because we are fearfully and wonderfully made! You have a wonderful and important destiny and purpose for each one of us! In Jesus' name, amen.*

DAY 2
THE SABBATH REST

> And on the seventh day God ended His work which He had done, and He rested on the seventh day from all His work which He had done. Then God blessed the seventh day and sanctified it, because in it He rested from all His work which God had created and made.
> —Genesis 2:2-3; read also Genesis 2

After God created the heavens and earth and everything in it in six days, He rested on the seventh day. In the Ten Commandments, He commanded us to do so as well. Rest must be a big issue to make the top ten commandments!

There are several reasons why this is so: First, it is a matter of obedience to God. He has commanded us to rest. Because the children of Israel did not obey God's commandments regarding the Sabbath rest, they were sent into captivity to Babylon.

Second, rest is an issue of trust in God. Cindy Jacobs says, "Vine's Old Testament concordance says that by resting, man witnessed his trust in God to give fruit to his labor. Perhaps when we continue to work without time off, we are saying to God, 'You cannot bless the fruit of my labor if I take time out.'"[1]

Third is that rest is for our physical, spiritual, and emotional well-being. God created us and He knows how much rest we need.

In our nation as we were growing up, except for church,

everyone stayed home on Sundays. No stores or gas stations were open. There were no sports or school activities because it was the Lord's Day. Sundays were the day we went to church, and then enjoyed family and friends. The Lord's Day was honored and respected.

We can see Jesus in this verse also because the Sabbath is a shadow of the rest available through the person and work of Jesus. *"There remains therefore a rest for the people of God. For he who has entered His rest has himself also ceased from his works as God did from His"* (Hebrews 4:9–10).

PRAYER

> *Help us, Lord, to enter into Your rest through faith and obedience. When we are tempted to work seven days a week, let us remember that on the Sabbath, you rested and commanded that we do the same! Amen.*

Genesis 1–Genesis 22

DAY 3

THE PLAN OF REDEMPTION

> And I will put enmity between you and the woman, and between your seed and her Seed; He shall bruise your head, and you shall bruise His heel.
> —GENESIS 3:15; READ ALSO GENESIS 3

THIS VERSE, GENESIS 3:15, is a very significant verse. It is the beginning of the gospel in the Old Testament. This was spoken right on the day of the fall of man.

This is speaking of Jesus, who would later crush the head of the enemy. The heel is the part within the serpent's reach. Jesus, in taking on humanity, brought Himself near to Satan's domain so Satan could strike Him. When Adam and Eve disobeyed God and ate the fruit in the garden, sin was introduced into the human race.

This prophecy also gives the first hint of the virgin birth, declaring the Messiah—the Deliverer—would be the Seed of the Woman but not of the man.

In Romans 5:19, we read, *"For as by one man's disobedience (Adam) many were made sinners, so also by one Man's obedience (Jesus Christ) many will be made righteous."* Then in Romans 6:23, we read, *"For the wages of sin is death, but the gift of God is eternal life through Christ Jesus our Lord."* Through these words, we see that God had a plan for our restoration from the very beginning through His Son, Jesus.

Julia Ward Howe wrote "The Battle Hymn of the Republic" after a visit to a Union Army camp in 1862. The

3rd verse of the song alluded to Genesis 3:15 when she wrote this: "I have read a fiery gospel writ in burnished rows of steel: 'As ye deal with my contemners (despised ones), so with you, my grace shall deal; Let the Hero, born of woman, crush the serpent with His heel, Since God is marching on.'"[2]

PRAYER

> *Thank You, Lord, that You had a plan to rescue, restore, and redeem us from the beginning of time. Your truth is marching on! Glory hallelujah! Come into our lives and hearts today and have Your way! Amen!*

Genesis 1–Genesis 22

DAY 4

WALKING WITH GOD

> And Enoch walked with God; and he
> was not, for God took him.
> —Genesis 5:24; read also Genesis 4–5

WALKING WITH GOD means walking by faith. *"For we walk by faith, not by sight"* (2 Corinthians 5:7). It also means walking in agreement with God. *"Can two walk together, unless they are agreed?"* (Amos 3:3). We must also walk in the light to have fellowship with God. *"But if we walk in the light as He is in the light, we have fellowship with one another, and the blood of Jesus Christ His Son cleanses us from all sin"* (1 John 1:7). Walking with God speaks of a true, deep relationship. After walking with God like this, God just took Enoch. One day God said, "You don't need to walk home. Why don't you just come home with Me?" Enoch and Elijah were the only two Old Testament saints that were translated.

Hebrews 11:5 tells us the foundation of Enoch's walk with God: "By faith Enoch was taken away so that he did not see death, 'and was not found, because God had taken him'; for before he was taken he had this testimony, that he pleased God."

After he begot Methuselah, Enoch walked with God. It seems he began to walk with God in a special way after the birth of Methuselah. The name Methuselah means, *"when he is dead, it shall come."* Enoch had a special awareness from God that judgment was coming at the birth of

Methuselah. This was one of the things that got him closer in his walk with God. Methuselah lived nine hundred and sixty-nine years and when he died the flood came.

Jude 14-15 tells us that Enoch was a prophet and could see the second coming of Jesus. *"Behold, the Lord comes with ten thousands of His saints, to execute judgment on all, to convict all who are ungodly."* He had revelation of the return of Jesus Christ.

PRAYER

> *How wonderful that there were signposts from the very beginning speaking of the rapture of the saints. Lord, help us to be ready for your second coming also. Help us to be people that "walk with God." Help us to walk in faith and have the testimony that "we pleased God!" In Jesus' name, amen.*

Genesis 1–Genesis 22

DAY 5
GOD'S COVENANT WITH NOAH

> But I will establish My covenant with you; and you shall go into the ark—you, your sons, your wife, and your sons' wives with you. And of every living thing of all flesh you shall bring two of every sort into the ark, to keep them alive with you; they shall be male and female.
> —Genesis 6:18-19; read also Genesis 6-9

Genesis chapters 6–9 contain the account of Noah and the flood. In Genesis 6:18, the word "covenant" is used in the Bible for the first time. God told Noah to build this huge boat in the middle of a dry country where it had never rained, and it took him over one hundred years to build it. It must have looked ridiculous.

God told Noah to build the ark because He was going to judge the people of the earth by sending a great flood that would cover the earth. As God looked upon the earth, He saw it was very corrupt and was filled with violence. The "sons of God" (rebellious angels) had taken the daughters of earth as wives and had children who were giants. "Satan tried to pollute the genetic pool of mankind with a satanic corruption, to…make the human race unfit for bringing forth the Seed of the woman—the Messiah promised in Genesis 3:15."[3] Jesus said in Luke 17:26 that in the last days it would be as in the days of Noah.

It rained forty days and forty nights and even the mountains were covered with water. After one year, the ark rested on the top of Mount Ararat and remains there to this day.[4]

After the flood subsided, Noah and his family and the animals left the ark (Genesis 8:18). Noah built an altar to the Lord. God made a covenant with Noah that He would never again curse the ground and destroy every living thing. As the sign of this covenant, God gave something that all men can still see in the sky—the rainbow. *"I set My rainbow in the cloud, and it shall be for the sign of the covenant between Me and the earth"* (Genesis 9:13).

PRAYER

> *Thank You, Lord, that Noah found grace in Your eyes. Thank You for the ark of safety You provided for Noah and thank You, Jesus, that You are our ark of safety. When the storms of life come, we can run to You! In Jesus' name, amen.*

DAY 6
PROMISES TO ABRAHAM

> Now the Lord had said to Abram: "Get out of your country, from your family and from your father's house, to a land that I will show you. I will make you a great nation; I will bless you and make your name great; and you shall be a blessing. I will bless those who bless you and I will curse him who curses you; and in you all the families of the earth shall be blessed."
> —Genesis 12:1-3; read also Genesis 10-12

THE CALLING OUT of Abraham in the above scripture, marks the beginning of the history of Israel. These three verses contain the declaration of what God intends to do in the whole world, and how He is going to do it. It is the first clear proclamation of the gospel, according to Paul's letter written to the Galatians: *"And the Scripture, foreseeing that God would justify the Gentiles (nations) by faith, preached the gospel to Abraham beforehand, saying, 'In you all the nations shall be blessed'"* (Galatians 3:8).

This amazing promise was fulfilled in the Messiah that came from Abraham's lineage. All the families of the earth would be blessed through Jesus. This also means that we, as children of Abraham, are to take this gospel to all the nations.

This covenant with Abraham promises him a land, a nation, and a great name. All who bless Israel will be blessed and all who curse Israel will be cursed. This remains true today. All nations that have been against Israel have been conquered or destroyed. For example, when Rome killed Paul and many others and destroyed Jerusalem under Titus, Rome soon fell. Poland fell after the pogroms; Hitler's Germany also went down after the slaughter of the Jews. When Britain refused access of the Jews during World War II, she lost her empire.

The United States has been a blessing to Israel and has been blessed. President Truman supported the creation of Israel. President Trump supported moving our embassy to Jerusalem.

PRAYER

> *Our Father in heaven, we praise You for Your great plan to bless all the nations of the earth through the Jews. They are Your chosen people through whom the Messiah came to earth. We bless them and pray for all of them to come to know their Messiah personally. In Jesus' name, amen.*

Genesis 1–Genesis 22

DAY 7

GOD'S COVENANT WITH ABRAHAM

> And it came to pass, when the sun went down and it was dark, that behold, there appeared a smoking oven and a burning torch that passed between those pieces. On the same day the LORD made a covenant with Abram, saying: "To your descendants I have given this land, from the river of Egypt to the great river, the River Euphrates---"
> —Genesis 15:17-18; read also Genesis 13-15

This is the first blood sacrifice covenant. This Abrahamic covenant is the Old Testament model for the New Covenant in Jesus Christ.

God had asked Abraham to bring Him a three-year-old heifer, a three-year-old female goat, a three-year old ram, a turtle dove, and a young pigeon. He then was instructed to cut them all in two, except the birds, and place the halves opposite each other.

Abraham knew that according to the custom of his time, God was asking him to get ready to sign a contract. The covenant was made when parties to the agreement walked through the animal parts together, repeating the terms of the covenant.

In this case God passed between those pieces by Himself as a smoking oven and a burning torch. The smoking oven reminds us of the pillar of cloud, and the torch reminds us of the pillar of fire in the wilderness. In a sense, the Father walked through the broken and bloody body of Jesus to establish His covenant with us, and God signed it for both of us.[5]

The covenant God made with Abraham was to give all the land from the river of Egypt to the great river, the River Euphrates, to Israel forever. Most important, this covenant was to be marked by the shedding of blood.

PRAYER

> *Thank You, Father, for the plan you had to redeem us from the beginning of time. Thank You for the picture in the Old Testament of the sacrifice of Your Son Jesus for us. Thank You for the forgiveness of sins through the blood of Jesus, for without the shedding of blood there can be no forgiveness (Hebrews 9:22). We praise You that as You were making this covenant with Abraham, You were thinking of us. In Jesus' name, amen.*

Genesis 1–Genesis 22

DAY 8
GOD REAFFIRMS THE COVENANT

> This is My covenant which you shall keep, between Me and you and your descendants after you: Every male child among you shall be circumcised...
> —Genesis 17:10; read also Genesis 16-17

A COVENANT IS A compact, pledge, treaty, or agreement. From the time of Adam to the time of Christ, Scripture is filled with accounts of how God entered into blood covenants with His people.

Accounts of blood covenants are not only found in Scripture, but in history; it is still practiced by many tribes today. The story is told of Henry Stanley, a journalist in the 1870's who traveled through the jungles of Africa in search of the missionary David Livingstone. On numerous occasions he observed the rite of blood-brotherhood to protect himself in his travels.

On one occasion he met Mirambo, a fierce warrior. They decided to make a covenant of friendship. As they sat facing each other on a straw carpet, an incision was made in each of their right legs, blood was extracted and interchanged. The chief captain performing the ceremony then exclaimed that anyone who broke this, would be destroyed.[6]

The sign of the covenant God made with Abraham was circumcision. The cutting and removal of the foreskin of every male among Abraham's descendants would mark them as those who were in the covenant. It was a sign that they would put no trust in the flesh. Also, because it deals with the organ of procreation, it was a reminder of the special seed of Abraham, which would ultimately bring the Messiah.

God honored the covenant so that even at his advanced age, Abraham was able to father a child. Sarah also was able to conceive, and they named their son Isaac.

PRAYER

> *Thank You Father for Your Son Jesus who shed His blood for us and said, "This cup is the new covenant in my blood. This do, as often as you drink it, in remembrance of Me. For as often as you eat this bread and drink this cup, you proclaim the Lord's death till He comes" (1 Corinthians 11:25-26). Amen.*

Genesis 1–Genesis 22

DAY 9

SODOM'S DEPRAVITY

Then the LORD rained brimstone and fire on Sodom and Gomorrah, from the LORD out of the heavens.
—Genesis 19:24; read also Genesis 18–19

THREE MEN CAME to Abraham in Mamre and were on their way to Sodom to destroy it. Two were angels and the other was Jesus in human form before His incarnation. Abraham intercedes for Sodom and God said if there were ten righteous, He would not destroy it. Sodom was where his nephew, Lot, lived.

When they arrived, Lot invited the two angels in, and said it was not safe for them to spend the night in the open square. After they were inside, the men of the city came and wanted to abuse them in a sadistic, homosexual manner. Homosexuality is the only reason given here for Sodom's judgment.

As these men pressed against the door the angels struck them with blindness so they could not find the door.

When the morning dawned, the angels urged Lot to take his wife and his two daughters and leave the city at once. When they hesitated, the angels grabbed their hands and led them outside the city. They said, *"Escape for your life! Do not look behind you nor stay anywhere in the plain. Escape to the mountains lest you be destroyed"* (Genesis 19:17).

After they had escaped to a small city called Zoar, the LORD rained brimstone and fire on Sodom and Gomorrah.

The LORD overthrew those cities, all the plain, all the inhabitants of the cities, and what grew on the ground. Lot's wife looked back and became a pillar of salt. One can still see that area from Masada in Israel.

In Luke 17:29-30, Jesus said, *"...but on the day that Lot went out of Sodom it rained fire and brimstone from heaven and destroyed them all. Even so will it be in the day when the Son of Man is revealed."* Jesus was explaining what life would be like here on earth when He returned.

PRAYER

> *Lord, as we see the signs all around us of Your soon return, we ask that You would deliver us from evil. Protect us from the enticements and deceptions of the world, that we may stand before You on that Judgment Day. May we live in constant expectancy of Your soon return! Amen!*

Genesis 1–Genesis 22

DAY 10

THE LORD WILL PROVIDE

> And Abraham called the name of the place, The-LORD-Will Provide; as it is said to this day, "In the Mount of the LORD it shall be provided."
> —Genesis 22:14; read also Genesis 20–22

THE STORY OF Abraham and Isaac in this chapter provides the amazing prophetic picture of God offering His only Son as a sacrifice for us. Every detail of this story is a prophetic picture of Jesus.

As God offered His only Son as a sacrifice for us, God asked Abraham to offer his only son, Isaac, as a burnt offering in the land of Moriah. As Abraham laid the wood for the offering on Isaac's back, so Jesus carried His cross to His crucifixion. The place where God told Abraham to sacrifice his son Isaac is the same place where God sacrificed His own Son in the hills of Moriah outside Jerusalem.

As they were going to the place of sacrifice, Isaac asked where the lamb was for the burnt offering. Abraham replied that God would provide for Himself the lamb. It is important to note that Abraham had said to his servants, *"...the lad and I will go yonder and worship, and we will come back to you"* (Genesis 22:5). In Hebrews 11:19 it says that Abraham had concluded that God was able to raise Isaac up, even from the dead, and symbolically that is exactly what happened. It was a type of Christ being raised from the dead. Abraham, by faith, knew God would raise him up.

As Abraham was about to offer his son, God commanded an angel to say to Abraham, *"Do not lay your hand on the lad, or do anything to him; for now I know that you fear God, since you have not withheld your son, your only son from Me"* (Genesis 22:12). This place was called Jehovah Jireh—the LORD will provide. The Lord provided a ram in the bushes for the offering!

PRAYER

> *Thank You, Father, that You blessed Abraham and all his seed because he was faithful to You and did not hold back even his only son. We know that Christ is the seed of Abraham and because we belong to Christ, we also are Abraham's seed and heirs to the blessing. Because Abraham was blessed in every way, so are we! In Jesus' name, amen.*

JOB

DAY 11

JOB'S FEAR

> For the thing I greatly feared has come upon me, and what I dreaded has happened to me.
> —Job 3:25; read also Job 1-3

There are two stages for a great drama in the book of Job. First, we see the earthly stage. Job was a blameless and upright man who feared God and shunned evil. He was extremely wealthy and had seven sons and three daughters. This man was the greatest of all the people of the East.

Second, we see the stage in heaven. The sons of God came to present themselves before the LORD. Among these angelic beings was Satan. This shows that these fallen angelic beings had access to the presence of God at this time.

God asks Satan if he had considered Job, that there was none like him on the earth, a blameless and upright man. Satan accused Job that the reason he feared God was that God had put a hedge around him. Satan is the accuser of the brethren, and he accuses the saints before God day and night (Revelation 12:10).

Satan brought calamity after calamity upon Job. In all this, Job did not sin or charge God with wrong. In

James 5:11 Job is commended as persevering, and that in the end he was blessed. After his catastrophic losses, God revealed His majesty, omnipotence, and goodness to Job and restored all that Satan had taken.

The Bible said that what Job had feared came upon him. Fear can open the door for the enemy. *"For God has not given us a spirit of fear, but of power and of love and of a sound mind"* (2 Timothy 1:7). This perhaps is one of the greatest lessons of this book. Over and over Jesus tells us to fear not! *"'Why are you fearful, O you of little faith?' Then he arose and rebuked the winds and the sea, and there was a great calm"* (Matthew 8:26).

PRAYER

> *Our Father in heaven, we praise You that You have authority over the storms in our life. You speak Your peace to every situation we face. Thank You for showing us who our true enemy is. We thank You for your great love and care for us. Right now, we cast all our cares on You for You care for us (1 Peter 5:7). In Jesus' name, amen.*

DAY 12

JOB COMPLAINS

> Therefore I will not restrain my mouth; I will speak in the anguish of my spirit; I will complain in the bitterness of my soul.
> —Job 7:11; read also Job 4-7

Job is being very honest with God about his suffering. He is saying, "Please God, just leave me alone. How have I wronged You?" Job had lost his children, his property, and his health. His wife had told him to curse God and die."

At times like these we need to turn to the word of God. In John 10:10 we read, *"The thief does not come except to steal, and to kill, and to destroy. I (Jesus) have come that they may have life, and that they may have it more abundantly."* Jesus comes to bring life.

Does it help to complain? Will that bring relief and help? No, it won't. *"I complained and my spirit was overwhelmed"* (Psalm 77:3). Complaining will cause us to be totally overwhelmed and immobilized by our circumstances. As impossible as it may sound, the Bible's solution is found in 1 Thessalonians 5:18: *"In everything give thanks; for this is the will of God in Christ Jesus for you."*

Paul and Virginia Weidman, and their small children, Paul Jr. and John, were called to be missionaries in a remote region of Upper Volta Africa. Paul Jr. (6 years old) contracted malaria and there was no medical doctor or hospital available to treat him. They had preached to the

Mossi people about Jesus and His healing power. From his sickbed, little Paul preached to the people: "Do not follow Satan's road, but follow God's road, for it alone leads to heaven through Jesus Christ our Lord."[7] His life and witness had a great impact on the Mossi people. He died *(the thief kills)*, but his parents stayed and planted other churches there.

Forty years later they returned to that place (now Burkino Faso) and learned that there were at that time 5,000 churches and 600,000 believers in that area. God had multiplied the seed sown.

PRAYER

> *Help us Lord to trust You when things happen that we do not understand. Help us to give thanks in faith that "all things work together for good to those who love God..." (Romans 8:28). We thank You that You are always a good Father! In Jesus' name, amen.*

DAY 13

THERE IS NO MEDIATOR

> For He is not a man, as I am, that I may answer Him, and that we should go to court together. Nor is there any mediator between us, who may lay his hand on us both.
> —JOB 9:32-33; READ ALSO JOB 8-10

Have you ever had a relationship problem where you felt like there was nothing you could say or do that could "fix" your relationship? Some broken relationships seem hopeless, but we have seen many completely healed through the power of prayer!

This is what Job felt like in his relationship with God. He felt unjustly treated by God, yet he felt there was no way to address the problem. Since he could not confront God with his troubling circumstances face to face, Job despaired of ever finding a satisfactory answer to his problem.

Job longed for someone to bridge the gap between him and God.

> Job needed someone to sort out the differences between him and God. His prior belief system did not do that; his experience did not do that; neither did the counsel of his friends. Recognizing this need, Job cried out for a mediator between himself and God. Here, then, was Job crying out for someone who could stand authoritatively between God and himself, and so create a way of meeting, a possibility of contact.[8]

We, however, are so blessed because we do know the greatest Mediator of all: Jesus Christ. *"For there is one God and one Mediator between God and men, the Man Christ Jesus"* (1 Timothy 2:5). The end of Job's dispute comes later, but the end of our dispute with God is available now in Christ Jesus! And He is also the answer to settling disagreements with one another!

PRAYER

> *Thank You Father that You sent a Mediator for us! He is the perfect One who can fully settle the case between You and us. He made peace between us through the Blood of the cross. Our sin separated us from You, and there was no bridge to reach You. But when we accepted Christ as a payment for our sin, He became the bridge between us. Amen.*

DAY 14

JOB TRUSTED GOD

> Though He slay me, yet will I trust Him.
> Even so, I will defend my own ways before
> Him. He also shall be my salvation.
> —JOB 13:15-16; READ ALSO JOB 11-13

THE FRUSTRATION OF Job prompted him to say, *"I desire to reason with God"* (Job 13:3). It was bad enough that Job could not make sense of his situation, but it was even worse when his friends insisted on their *own wrong answer* to Job's crisis. They were determined Job suffered because he had greatly sinned.

When he said, *"Though he slay me, yet will I trust Him"* (v. 15), he was saying that even if my life is destroyed by this affliction, yet I hope that when this trial is over I will come forth as gold.

> Writing fictionally in the voice of a senior demon instructing a junior demon in his popular book *The Screwtape Letters,* C.S. Lewis stated – from a demon's perspective – this dynamic of trial in the life of the believer: "He (God) wants them to learn to walk and must therefore take away His hand; and if only the will to walk is really there He is pleased even with their stumbles. Do not be deceived, Wormwood. Our cause is never more in danger than when a human, no longer desiring, but still intending, to do our Enemy's will, looks round upon a universe from which every trace of Him

seems to have vanished, and asks why he has been forsaken, and still obeys."[9]

Another example of trusting God is in the book of Daniel. His friends, Shadrach, Meshach, and Abed-Nego, would not bow down to the gold image set up by King Nebuchadnezzar. The penalty for not bowing down was to be thrown into the burning fiery furnace. The three Hebrew men said, "Our God is able to deliver us, but if He doesn't, we will not serve your gods, nor will we worship the gold image which you have set up" (Daniel 3:17-18). The Lord miraculously delivered them and the king saw a fourth Man like the Son of God walking in the fire with them!!

PRAYER

> *Lord, we know that You know full well what it means to suffer for righteousness' sake. You trusted God while You were slain for our sins. Help us to trust You no matter what we go through. In Jesus' Name. Amen.*

DAY 15

HOPE

Where then is my hope? As for my hope, who can see it?
—Job 17:15; read also Job 14-17

Hope is an inner image of an eager expectation. Job had lost his hope. The Word of God is the answer for hopelessness.

There are three things which hope does:

- It sees beyond circumstances to what He has promised. In 2 Kings 6, the king of Syria had told his servants to go and find Elisha so he could send for him. When Elisha's servant saw the Syrians surround the city, he asked Elisha what they could do. Elisha prayed that God would open the eyes of his servant so he could see that there were more for them than against them. He saw that there were chariots of fire all around Elisha.

- It expects beyond circumstances. In Acts 27 as Paul was on his way to Rome and was caught in a huge storm at sea, the angel of God said not to be afraid. He told Paul that he would appear before Caesar and everyone on the ship would be saved.

- It rejoices beyond the circumstances. In 2 Chronicles 20, as the Israelites faced the army of the Ammonites, Moabites, and Mount Seir, the prophet said: *"Believe in the LORD your God, and you shall be established; believe His prophets, and you shall prosper"* (v. 20). Then they sent the worshippers out ahead of the army saying, *"Praise the LORD, For His mercy endures forever"* (v. 21), and the enemy was defeated.

PRAYER

Thank You Lord, that You are our hope. We pray Romans 15:13: "Now may the God of hope fill you with all joy and peace in believing, that you may abound in hope by the power of the Holy Spirit." We do praise You for turning around that hopeless-looking situation in our life. We know that nothing is impossible for You. Nothing is too hard for the Lord! We will praise You in advance before we see the miracle that You are going to do!! We are expecting miracles in our family, our church, our city and in our nation!! In Jesus' Name. Amen.

DAY 16

I KNOW THAT MY REDEEMER LIVES

> For I know that my Redeemer lives, and He shall stand at last on the earth; and after my skin is destroyed, this I know, that in my flesh I shall see God. Whom I shall see for myself, and my eyes shall behold, and not another. How my heart yearns within me!
> —JOB 19:25-27 READ ALSO JOB 18-21

JOB IS POSSIBLY the oldest book written. Many commentators feel that Job was written by Moses and that Moses' father-in-law Jethro told him Job's outstanding testimony.

These verses are a brilliant flash of faith in Job's otherwise dark and bleak background of crisis and suffering. Perhaps as he considered that future generations would indeed look at his life and words, it stirred him to a triumphant proclamation of faith.

The word translated *"Redeemer"* is one of the most wonderful concepts of the Old Testament. A redeemer was a vindicator of one unjustly wronged. He was a defender of the oppressed, a champion of the suffering. He had the responsibility to 'buy back' and so redeem the lost inheritance of a deceased relative.[10]

Who did Job see? He saw Jesus. What did he see? The resurrection. As we consider that the oldest book of the Bible has a revelation of Jesus Himself as Redeemer, we see the scarlet cord of redemption from the beginning of the Bible to the end.

In his early twenties, Benjamin Franklin, one of America's renowned Founding Fathers, wrote this epitaph reminiscent of the words of Job:

> The body of Benjamin Franklin, Printer, (Like the cover of an old book, its contents torn out and stripped of its lettering and gilding,) lies here, food for worms. But the work shall not be lost; for it will, as he believ'd, appear once more in a new and more elegant edition, Revised and Corrected by the Author.[11]

PRAYER

> *Jesus, you are the Resurrection and the Life. We thank You that we can have great faith that our lives count for something, and that there will be an eternity with You. Thank You that You have redeemed us from poverty, sickness and death. Because He lives, we can face tomorrow. Because He lives, all fear is gone. Because He lives we will live with Him forever! In Jesus' Name. Amen.*

DAY 17

AUTHORITY IN DECREES

> You will also declare a thing, and it will be established for you; so light will shine on your ways.
> —JOB 22:28; READ ALSO JOB 22-24

A DECLARATION IS AN official order, edict, or decision. This verse is a powerful tool in prayer, as God has given each believer authority to bring God's kingdom here on earth. Jesus prayed, *"Your kingdom come, Your will be done on earth as it is in heaven"* (Luke 11:2).

As kings make decrees, we, too, must make decrees for we are made *"kings and priests"* unto God according to Revelation 1:6.

Even David in the Old Testament understood this. There is no record of David asking God to help him when He faced Goliath. He simply decreed that God would assist him and declared what he was going to do to the giant. He declared to the giant, *"This day the LORD will deliver you into my hand and I will strike you and take your head from you... Then all this assembly shall know that the LORD does not save with sword and spear; for the battle is the LORD'S and He will give you into our hands"* (1 Samuel 17:46-47).

In 1980 Dutch Sheets was asked to pray for a newborn baby with a fractured skull. During the birth process the doctor had used forceps and had inadvertently fractured his skull. As Dutch began to pray, the Holy Spirit led him to command healing into the infant's skull. He decreed in the powerful name of Jesus that the baby's skull was being healed.

It happened instantly! Through this miracle the mother was born-again and at church the following Sunday he had the privilege of dedicating the baby to Jesus.[12]

We, too, have experienced miracles by decreeing according to this verse. Several times as my husband faced death during a time of dizzy spells, I decreed resurrection life, and the Lord heard and answered!!

PRAYER

> *We decree life today for those experiencing difficult and even life-threatening circumstances. We decree health and a complete turnaround in every circumstance not lining up with Your Word. In Jesus' Name. Amen.*

DAY 18

THE GIFT OF RIGHTEOUSNESS

> How then can man be righteous before God? Or how can he be pure who is born of a woman?
> —JOB 25:4; READ ALSO JOB 25-28

How many of us like gifts? The Bible talks about a wonderful gift for all of us in Romans 5:17: *"For if by the one man's offense death reigned through the one, much more those who receive abundance of grace and of the GIFT OF RIGHTEOUSNESS will reign in life through the One, Jesus Christ."* Job did not know that the answer to his question was a gift that only Jesus could give.

Righteousness simply defined is "right standing with God." It gives you the ability to be free of guilt, condemnation, fear, and inferiority. These four problems rob many Christians of God's blessings.

Righteousness is actually received at salvation. Because many have not understood the righteousness of God which is by faith, they have failed to experience the full joy of God's gift.

The message of righteousness is good news. The moment you hear this word, it should cause faith to rise up in your heart. *"If you confess with your mouth the Lord Jesus and believe in your heart that God has raised Him from the dead, you will be saved. For with the heart one believes unto righteousness, and with the mouth confession is made unto salvation"* (Romans 10:9-10).

This means you are freed from sin, with all its guilt and

condemnation. You are also freed from fear and inferiority. We are now "*heirs of God and joint heirs with Christ*" (Romans 8:17).

If we miss the mark and sin, 1 John 1:9 says: "*If we confess our sins, He is faithful and just to forgive us our sins and to cleanse us from all unrighteousness.*" We can now enter boldly into His presence with our praises and petitions.

PRAYER

> *Our Father who is in heaven, we give You thanks for showing us in Your Word how we can be made righteous. You were made sin for us that we might become the righteousness of God in Christ (2 Corinthians 5:21). Father, I ask You to forgive my sins, and purify my heart. I receive by faith, Your gift of righteousness through the Blood of Your Son. Amen.*

DAY 19

THE RIGHTEOUSNESS OF NATIONS

I put on righteousness and it clothed me; My
justice was like a robe and a turban.
—Job 29:14; read also Job 29-31

In George Washington's first presidential address, given 232 years ago, in 1789, he spoke this prophetic warning: "The propitious smiles of heaven cannot be expected on a nation that disregards the eternal rules of order and right that heaven itself has ordained." As long as the early colonists looked to God and appealed to heaven, they saw a great victory over the largest navy in the world from England.[13]

Then again in 1917, Woodrow Wilson stated that unless America threw its weight into World War 1, Western civilization itself could be destroyed. This excerpt from a speech given in 1911 is his view of the Word of God in society:

> There are great problems before the American people. There are problems which will need purity of spirit and an integrity of purpose such as has never been called for before in the history of this country. I should be afraid to go forward if I did not believe that there lay at the foundation of all our schooling and of all our thought this incomparable and unimpeachable Word of God. If we cannot

derive our strength thence, there is no source from which we can derive it...

No great nation can ever survive its own temptations and its own follies that does not indoctrinate its children in the Word of God; so that as schoolmaster and as Governor I know that my feet must rest with the feet of my fellowmen upon this foundation, and upon this foundation only; for the righteousness of nations, like the righteousness of men, must take its source from these foundations of inspiration.[14]

John Adams said also, "Our Constitution was made only for a moral and religious people. It is wholly inadequate to the government of any other."[15]

PRAYER

Father in heaven, as long as America remains, give us leaders who fear You and obey Your Word. We pray this in Jesus' name. Amen!

DAY 20

SET YOUR WORDS IN ORDER BEFORE ME

> If you can answer me, set your words in order before me; take your stand.
> —Job 33:5; read also Job 32-35

In the beginning of the book of Job we see Satan accusing Job before God. As we consider the words of "Job's comforters," we understand that this same spirit of accusation is at work. We see this in Elihu's comments: *"What man is like Job, who drinks scorn like water, who goes in company with the workers of iniquity, and walks with wicked men. For he has said, 'It profits a man nothing that he should delight in God'"* (Job 34:7-9).

Jesus, on the other hand is always our intercessor who is for us. Ed Silvoso learned this as God dealt with him when he was praying for his lost neighbors:

> I told God about everything that was wrong with these people. I talked to Him in disgust about the unwed mother and how she had to change because she was such a bad example to my daughters. I demanded that He do something about the couple who kept us awake at night with their arguing and fighting. I complained about the depressive neighbor whose front yard was a disgrace and a bane to real estate values on our block. And of course, I did not forget about the teenager on drugs. I made it

perfectly clear to the Lord what a detriment this young man was to our neighborhood.

All of a sudden I sensed God saying, "Ed I am so glad you have not witnessed to any of these yet, . . because I don't want your neighbors to know that you and I are related. I hurt when they hurt. I reach out to them. I love them but you don't...Unless you love them, I cannot trust you with their lives."[16]

Ed was lining up with the "Accuser of the brethren" rather than Jesus, our Intercessor. He repented and has become a great soul winner!

PRAYER

Lord, help us always to line up our words and thoughts with You as we speak to and about people. You loved us so much that You died for us. You are for us, not against us. You desire to give us a future and a hope. You see us through eyes of faith as to what we are becoming in You. Amen!!

DAY 21

EXCELLENT IN POWER

> With God is awesome majesty. ... He is excellent in power, in judgment and abundant justice; He does not oppress.
> —JOB 37:22B-23; READ ALSO JOB 36-37

JUST AS ELIHU proclaims God's power, majesty, and excellence, we also will praise Him today for His excellent glory!! Because we are children of the Almighty God, excellence is our spiritual DNA also!! We are born of incorruptible seed "by the word of God" (1 Peter 1:23). We are joint heirs with Jesus and partners in His ministry, which was and is a ministry of excellence (2 Corinthians 5:18).

We have an excellent heritage! We have heroes like Daniel in our spiritual tree. Talk about someone who was not content to do just enough to get by! Even as a captive living in Babylon, Daniel did such a first-class job at everything he was given to do, that the Bible says: "Daniel was preferred above the presidents and princes, because an excellent spirit was in him; and the king thought to set him over the whole realm. So, this Daniel prospered" (Daniel 6:3, 28).[17]

If God could do that for Daniel, should we not also be prospering and being promoted to the highest place available in whatever sphere of influence to which God has called us?

Job also was commended by the brother of Jesus because of his excellence in patience and endurance when he wrote: "*Indeed we count them blessed who endure. You* have heard of the perseverance of Job and seen the end intended by the Lord—that the Lord is very compassionate and merciful"* (James 5:11).

We are never to offer up a "half-baked" job to the Lord!!! The Bible says: *"And whatever you do, do it heartily, as to the Lord and not to men"* (Colossians 3:23). We must do everything with excellence!

PRAYER

> *Father in heaven, You are a God of excellence in love, power and majesty. How could we even think of doing anything for You and not put our whole hearts into it! Help us never to stoop to mediocrity as we are serving you. We always want to do our very best for you!! In Jesus' Name. Amen.*

DAY 22

THE OMNIPOTENCE OF GOD

> Where were you when I laid the foundations of the earth? Tell Me, if you have understanding. Who determined its measurements? Surely you know! Or who stretched the line upon it? To what were its foundations fastened? Or who laid its cornerstone, when the morning stars sang together, and all the sons of God shouted for joy?
> —Job 38:4-7; read also Job 38-42

This is one of the most amazing passages in the Bible when God is asking Job questions. *"Did you help me make the crocodile?...Were you there when I created the earth?...Did you shut in the sea with doors and tell it: this far you may come, but no farther and here your proud waves must stop?...Did you set the wild donkey free?...Do you know anything about the elephant?...The leviathan? . ."* (Chapters 38-41).

When Job said, "No," then God said that he should stop giving advice and talking about things he did not know anything about.

At this point Job did not give excuses. He could have said, "Well, get rid of these nasty friends and I could be a human being." Or, "What about my wife? You know she told me to curse God and die."

No, he said, "I abhor myself." He saw that he had gotten into self-righteousness. He repented, and God forgave him. Then God asked him to pray for his friends. He could have said, "What? Those friends? They're not friends, they are thugs!"

Job did the right thing. He repented and then he forgave his friends. When Job prayed for them, God turned his captivity around. He received double finances, ten more children, his health returned, and God doubled his years.

It was a nine-month trial. He was 70 when he went into this trial, and God gave him 70 more years, a total of 140 years!

PRAYER

> *Thank you Lord for this wonderful story of righteous Job. We believe that we, too, will get double for our trouble as we trust in You. Help us to repent for our self-righteousness and forgive friends that accuse us wrongly. We praise You that You will never let us down!! In Jesus' Name. Amen.*

GENESIS 23-GENESIS 50

DAY 23

THE WOMAN AT THE WELL

> Praised be Yahweh, the God of Abraham, for you have faithfully kept your promise to my master and displayed your wonderful kindness and love. Yahweh, you led me straight to the very place of my master's relatives!
> —Genesis 24:27 TPT. Read also Genesis 23-24

After Sarah died, Abraham buried her at Hebron in the land of Canaan. After this, Abraham sought for a wife for Isaac. He did not want him to marry a Canaanite, but he wanted his servant, Eliezer to go to his native land and find a wife from his relatives. However, Eliezer was not ever to take Isaac back to his native land.

Eliezer promised and then left for Mesopotamia where Abraham's brother Nahor had lived. While he was there, he prayed that the future wife of Isaac would be the one who would draw water for him and for the camels.

When Rebekah, the granddaughter of Nahor saw him, she quickly lowered her jar to give him a drink, and then drew water for all his camels.

Would she be willing to give ten thirsty camels water from the well? The woman's willingness to serve water showed that she had a true servant-spirit; one camel can drink twenty gallons!! It would take an exceptional woman to do something like this.

This one act of service qualified her to be Isaac's wife, and to be brought into the line of Christ and His inheritance. She is a picture of the servant-bride of Jesus Christ.[18]

Sometimes we do not realize how one act of humble service will affect the world and bring promotion to our own life. From this act of service, she was given many gifts and went with the servant back to Canaan. It was love at first sight for Isaac. He married her and was greatly comforted after his mother's death.

PRAYER

> *Thank you Lord, that Your plans for us are so amazing! Each day is so important!! Rebekah had no idea she was going to leave on a journey across the world the next day to fulfill Your plans and become part of the lineage of Jesus Christ! Help us to walk so closely to You today, that we will not miss Your divine appointments!! In Jesus' Name. Amen.*

Genesis 23–Genesis 50

DAY 24
THE BIRTHRIGHT WAS VALUABLE

Thus Esau despised his birthright.
—Genesis 25:34b; read also Genesis 25-26

AFTER TWENTY YEARS, Isaac and Rebekah were blessed with twin boys: Esau and Jacob. These two boys had totally different characters. Esau was a skilled hunter, whom Isaac loved, but Jacob was more contemplative and content to stay close to home. Rebekah loved him the best.

One day Esau came in from the field and he was famished. When he smelled the food Jacob was cooking, he was desperate to eat some. Jacob said he had to trade his birthright to get some. Esau said, "Look, I am about to die; so what is this birthright to me?"

Jacob knew that the birthright was valuable, and he wanted it. The son of the birthright received a double portion of the inheritance, became the head of the family and the spiritual leader upon the passing of the father. In this case it meant he would inherit the covenant God made with Abraham, the covenant of a land, a nation, and the Messiah.

Esau thought he would die one day anyway, so what good was this birthright to him? Is this like some of us today? Do we choose sin for a season rather that the joys of God forever? In Ephesians 1:3-14, we are shown the treasury of riches that are ours by birthright in Jesus: every spiritual blessing; the blessing of being chosen in Jesus; adoption into God's family; true and total forgiveness; the riches of God's grace; an eternal inheritance; the guarantee of the indwelling Holy Spirit.[19]

Will we be like Esau and trade what is valuable for something momentary like a bowl of stew? Will we leave God out of our priorities? Heaven forbid!!

PRAYER

> *Dear Father in heaven, help us always to choose our priorities carefully. Help us to consider our spiritual birthright in Christ and how important it really is. Through You, Jesus, we have complete acceptance! Through You, we have been made rich in every way! Through You we have access to eternal life! In Jesus' Name. Amen.*

Genesis 23–Genesis 50

DAY 25
THE ANOINTED STONE

> He took a stone from there, made it his pillow, and lay down to sleep. He had a dream of a stairway securely fixed on the earth and reaching into heaven.
> —Genesis 28:11b-12a, TPT; read also Genesis 27-28

After Jacob deceived Isaac and took Esau's blessing of the firstborn son, he escaped from his brother and fled to Haran, the home of Rebekah's family in Mesopotamia. Rebekah and Isaac did not want Jacob to marry a Canaanite woman.

On the way, he set up camp at Bethel. He took a stone, made it his pillow, and lay down to sleep. Perhaps this was one of the stones of the altar erected by Abraham (Genesis 12:8).

> Jesus is the anointed Stone on whom we lay our head. To lay your head (thoughts and dreams) on Him is to discover the beauty of God. When the anointing of Jesus fills our head (mind), we will see heaven opened with fresh revelation and perceive the visions of God. Jesus is the Chief Corner Stone, the Stone that killed Goliath, and the Stone of Daniel Chapter 2:34 and 45 that conquers kingdoms.[20]

While Jacob was sleeping, he had a dream and saw a stairway reaching from earth to heaven. He saw angels ascending and descending on the stairway. (In John 1:51

we see the angels ascending and descending upon Jesus. He is the ladder.)[21] God spoke to him and told him He was the God of Abraham and Isaac, and that the land he was lying on would be given to him and his countless descendants. One of those descendants would be the Messiah. Notice that when God spoke to him, he did not scold him for being a deceiver. He revealed Himself as the One who would never leave or forsake him.

PRAYER

> *Thank You, Lord that You can see beyond our sins and shortcomings and can see what You are going to make of our lives. Thank you for Your patience and love. If you can take a deceiver like Jacob and turn his name to Israel, father of the twelve tribes, then you can take us and make something beautiful out of our lives as well!! In Jesus' Name. Amen.*

Genesis 23–Genesis 50

DAY 26

SOWING AND REAPING

> Then Jacob kissed Rachel, and lifted
> up his voice and wept.
> —GENESIS 29:11; READ ALSO GENESIS 29-30

WHEN JACOB ARRIVED in Haran, he met beautiful Rachel, his cousin, and fell deeply in love with her. He served his uncle Laban seven years in exchange for Rachel, but on his wedding night Laban tricked Jacob by bringing his older daughter Leah into Jacob's tent.

Jacob was shocked to see Leah lying next to him in the morning. Laban, his father-in-law said it was not the custom to give the younger daughter in marriage before the older daughter was married. After the bridal week, he was given Rachel as a wife, but he had to serve Laban another seven years.

> For those seven years, God was teaching Jacob submission to the rights of the firstborn. It was not right to marry the younger before the firstborn. All that Jacob circumvented in stealing the blessing from Esau, he now must learn by serving another for seven years and learn the timing of God. After the seven years were over, Laban tricked Jacob by giving him Leah, not Rachel on his wedding night. Jacob was fooled by the veil over the bride thinking it was Rachel, even as he had fooled his father with a hairy skin over his arms, confusing him with Esau. Every

"Jacob" will one day meet his "Laban."[22] Because he sowed deception, that is what he reaped.

Jacob loved Rachel, but she remained childless. When God saw that Leah was unloved, he opened her womb and gave her six sons. The fourth son was Judah who was the ancestor of Jesus.

PRAYER

Dear Heavenly Father, we see that You are a merciful and loving heavenly Father. Jacob did reap what he sowed, but You blessed him abundantly and gave him twelve sons who became the twelve tribes of Israel. We give You praise for forgiving him and doing exceedingly abundantly above all he could ask or think of You, and You will do the same for us. In Jesus' Name. Amen.

DAY 27
JACOB SEEKS THE BLESSING

> So Jacob called the name of the place Peniel: "For I have seen God face to face, and my life is preserved."
> —GENESIS 32:30; READ ALSO GENESIS 31-32

AFTER ALL OF Jacob's family and flocks had crossed over the brook, he was left alone on the east side of the Jordan. It was here where a Man wrestled with him. This was a special appearance of Jesus in the Old Testament before His incarnation in Bethlehem. The Man wrestled with Jacob all night.

As the wrestling match continued, Jacob sought the blessing with weeping. He knew he was defeated, yet he desperately wanted a blessing from this Greater One. In the past, he never felt the need to trust God alone. He could scheme and figure things out himself.

Before he could be delivered from Esau, whom he feared would kill him, he had to be delivered from his own self-will and self-reliance. His real enemy was not Esau, but it was his own carnal fleshly nature, which had not been conquered by God.

"*So He said to him, 'What is your name?' He said, 'Jacob.' And He said, 'Your name shall no longer be called Jacob, but Israel; for you have struggled with God and with men, and have prevailed'*" (Genesis 32:27-28).

After this, the Man blessed him. This was the blessing of the passing of the old (Jacob) life, and the coming of a new (Israel) life. He blessed him at the place of special trial and testing; of intense pleading to God; of conscious weakness; of seeing the face of God.[23] Jacob called that place Peniel and said that he had seen the face of God and lived.

He also received a perpetual limp and would remember his being conquered by God for the rest of His life.

PRAYER

> *Lord, help us to remember Paul's words from Galatians 2:20: "I have been crucified with Christ; it is no longer I who live, but Christ lives in me; and the life which I now live in the flesh I live by faith in the Son of God, who loved me and gave Himself for me." Help us to yield our old carnal nature to You and receive Your new nature. In Jesus' Name. Amen.*

Genesis 23–Genesis 50

DAY 28
PROMISES KEPT

> And he built an altar there and called the place
> El Bethel, because there God appeared to him
> when he fled from the face of his brother.
> —GENESIS 35:7; READ ALSO GENESIS 33-35

AFTER THE TRAGEDY at Shechem concerning Jacob's daughter Dinah, God told Jacob to go at once to Bethel, which means "the House of God." This is where Jacob had the dream of the ladder extending to heaven with angels ascending and descending on it; he was fleeing from his brother Esau. God spoke to him at that place and told him that the land on which he lay would be given to him and his descendants as he had promised Abraham and Isaac.

Thirty years later God spoke to him to go to Bethel and build an altar to God. He was telling him to resume a life of worship there. This would be a wonderful example to his children.

Jacob said to his household to get rid of every foreign god and purify themselves and change their clothes. The change of garments symbolizes a change of character. Jude 23 says: "*but others save with fear, pulling them out of the fire, hating even the garment defiled by the flesh.*" Jacob's family got right with God after Jacob did himself. This shows the tremendous leadership role men have within the family.

When they came to Bethel perhaps Jacob looked upon

those stones among which he had lain down to sleep as a lonely man. This was where Jacob vowed to God that if He would be with him and keep him and give him bread to eat and clothing to put on, so that he could come to his father's house in peace, then the Lord would be his God. Jacob kept his promise (Genesis 28:20-22).

God reiterated His promise to Jacob, that his name would now be Israel, and that the land which He gave to Abraham and Isaac He was giving to Jacob. He told him he would be the ancestor of kings. One of those kings was King Jesus.

PRAYER

> *Dear Father, You are the God who protects us and brings your promises to pass in our lives. Even when we fail You, You never leave us or forsake us. We want to build an altar to You in our hearts and thank You for Your faithfulness!! In Jesus' Name. Amen.*

Genesis 23–Genesis 50

DAY 29

THE STORY OF JOSEPH

So he said to them, "Please hear this
dream which I have dreamed."
—GENESIS 37:6; READ ALSO GENESIS 36-38

WHEN JOSEPH WAS seventeen, his father made him a richly ornamented robe. When his brothers saw it, they realized that his father loved him more than them and they hated him.

Then he began having dreams which caused his brothers to hate him even more. In the first one he dreamed that they were binding sheaves of grain in the field, and his sheaf rose up and stood upright. Then his brothers' sheaves gathered around his and bowed down to his! In the second dream the sun and moon and eleven stars were bowing down to him. Even his father asked if he really thought that his parents and brothers were going to come and bow to the ground before him! These dreams had a profound effect on Joseph. If you dreamed the stars of heaven were bowing down to you, do you not think it would affect you? Joseph behaved with excellence because he saw himself as a "star."[24]

One day his father asked him to go to his brothers who were in Dothan. When they saw him, they said, *"Here comes this dream expert. Let's kill him and throw his body into one of these dry wells. We can say that a wild animal ate him. Then we'll see how his dreams turn out"* (Genesis 37:19-20 TPT).

They decided to throw him into a dry, empty pit instead.

When some Ishmaelite merchants came by on their way to Egypt, they sold him for twenty pieces of silver. He was sold to Potiphar, one of Pharaoh's officials.

The brothers dipped Joseph's coat into goat's blood and showed their father who thought a wild animal must have killed him.

PRAYER

> *Father in heaven, we are amazed at the timing of Your plans. You protected Joseph from the hatred of his brothers and had the Ishmaelites come by at the perfect time for Joseph to go with them. You were going to need him to be in Egypt to save his family and nation when the famine came. You also have us in Your perfect timing. Help us to trust You with the details of our lives—especially when we don't understand. Amen!*

Genesis 23–Genesis 50

DAY 30
JOSEPH, A TYPE OF CHRIST

> The LORD was with Joseph, and he was a successful man; and he was in the house of his master the Egyptian.
> —Genesis 39:2; read also Genesis 39-40

It seems that Joseph excelled in everything. Potiphar, who purchased Joseph, realized that God's presence was with Joseph and that was why everything he did prospered. Potiphar placed everything he owned under Joseph's oversight, and the Lord blessed the Egyptian's house.

Joseph could have complained about being sold by his brothers into slavery and have had a very bad attitude about being Potiphar's slave. However, it seems that Joseph wanted to be a successful slave. His attitude was like Jesus; *"For the Son of Man did not come to be served, but to serve"* (Matthew 20:28).

After Potiphar's wife falsely accused Joseph of sexual sin, he was thrown in prison, and remained there two years. Like Jesus was falsely accused and was silent before His accusers, so Joseph did not defend himself either. Joseph suffered for someone else's sin, even as Jesus was punished for our sins. There are many parallels in the life of Joseph and Jesus.

Even in prison he found favor in the sight of the keeper of the prison who committed all the prisoners to Joseph's hand. All this proved to be a training ground to develop administrative skills to one day save his family and to save the whole world. This, too, shows Joseph as a type of Christ.

PRAYER

Father in heaven, we pray that we could follow this wonderful example of a righteous man who continued to trust You in spite of difficult circumstances!! He went from privilege in his father's house to the pit where his brothers threw him. From there he went to the slave market. After serving as a slave for eleven years he went to prison unjustly for two more years. And yet, wherever he went he was successful and prosperous. Even after interpreting the dreams of the baker and butler accurately, he was still forgotten. In all this he did not complain. Help us to follow in his example of patience in times of testing and see how You blessed him abundantly above all he could have ever asked or thought. Just like you brought Joseph through, You will bring us through!! In Jesus' Name. Amen.

Genesis 23–Genesis 50

DAY 31
FROM THE PIT TO THE PALACE

> Then Pharaoh said to Joseph, "Inasmuch as God has shown you all this, there is no one as discerning and wise as you."
> —Genesis 41:39; read also Genesis 41-42

Joseph's dreams landed him in a pit and later in a prison. It was his gift for interpreting dreams that brought him out of prison to stand before Pharaoh.

Pharaoh had two disturbing dreams. In the first one seven cows, fine looking and fat fed in the meadow. Then, seven other cows ugly and gaunt, ate up the fat cows. In the second dream seven heads of grain, plump and good were eaten up by seven thin heads. How upsetting that no one could interpret them. That is, until the butler remembered Joseph who had correctly interpreted his dream (Chapter 40). Pharaoh brought Joseph out of prison, and he gave the interpretation: there would be seven years of plenty, followed by seven years of famine. Joseph said officers needed to store up food in the seven good years to provide for the seven years of famine. In one day, he was promoted to being second in command to Pharaoh.

Joseph was a forerunner of our Lord Jesus:

> Rejected by his brethren, refused by those to whom he was sent, falsely accused and condemned, classed with the wicked, thrust into prison, rescuing one of his poor associates, called to a throne, it would be possible

in almost every particular to substitute the name of Jesus for that of Joseph.[25]

Joseph was now thirty years old. This is the age at which Jesus began his earthly ministry. Nevertheless, it is a very young age to be awarded the highest governmental position in a powerful nation with the responsibility of running its affairs!

PRAYER

> *Father in heaven, it is so wonderful to read of Your wisdom being given to a young man like Joseph who was rejected by his own family but accepted by You and who fulfilled Your purposes in his generation. May we, like Joseph, fulfill the purposes for our generation, and walk in wisdom, love and forgiveness. In Jesus' Name. Amen.*

DAY 32
THE DREAMS COME TO PASS

> So it was God, not you, who sent me here.
> —Genesis 45:8a TPT; read also Genesis 43-45

IN FOLLOWING THIS exciting story about Joseph, we see that indeed Joseph's brothers came to Egypt to get grain during the famine. And yes, they all bowed down to him as in the first dream of the sheaves bowing down to him. Since Benjamin was not in that first group, Joseph required that Benjamin return with them. Again, they all bowed down to him. Joseph revealed himself to them and all the brothers were shocked and even terrified that it was actually Joseph their brother!! He then sent them back to get their father so the whole family could be taken care of in Egypt.

Let's take a look at how Joseph was a type of Christ in this narrative:

- This perhaps is a picture of what will happen when the Jewish people see Jesus for who He is when He returns. They will *"mourn for him as one mourns for his only son"* (Zechariah 12:10).

- *"So now it was not you who sent me here, but God"* (v. 8). His words flowed from a loving, forgiving heart as his kindness washed over them. Through his tears he persuaded them that God was using him to preserve their lives. Though they did not realize it, Joseph's brothers were helping the Lord fulfill his promise to Abraham that through his seed (Jesus), all the world would be blessed.

- As Jehovah Rohi, he settled them in Goshen so that they would be near him as a loving shepherd (v. 10).

- As Jehovah Jireh provides all our needs, Joseph would provide all their needs so they would not live in poverty (v. 11).

PRAYER

Father in heaven, help us to see beyond the difficulties and sorrows of the present, to Your higher purposes. Help us to trust and praise You when we cannot see exactly what You are doing. If Joseph's family had not been brought to Egypt, they would have assimilated into the pagan tribes of Canaan and lost their distinctiveness as a nation. You truly are a God who works all things out for our good! In Jesus' Name. Amen.

Genesis 23–Genesis 50

DAY 33

ISRAEL AND FAMILY MOVE TO EGYPT

> So He said, "I am God, the God of your father; do not fear to go down to Egypt, for I will make of you a great nation there."
> —Genesis 46:3; read also Genesis 46-48

Think of moving to a foreign country at the age of one hundred and thirty-seven years! God spoke words of comfort to him saying, *"I will go with you to Egypt, and I will bring your descendants back to this land. And the hand of Joseph will be there to close your eyes when you die"* (Genesis 46:4 TPT).

What an emotional reunion that was when Jacob and Joseph laid eyes on each other after twenty years! The great Egyptian ruler was once more only a boy needing his father. The son Jacob thought was dead was alive and ruled over Egypt!

The family settled in Goshen, the choicest part of Egypt with their flocks and herds. They had food during the famine. God gave Joseph the wisdom not only to feed the people that came there, but he made Egypt rich. In time, Egypt gave it back to God's people—with interest.

When the time of Israel's death drew near, he made Joseph promise to not bury him in Egypt, but to bury him where his fathers were, in the field of Machpelah near Mamre (Hebron).

Why was this so important? Jacob was looking forward to the time of resurrection! Abraham, Isaac, and Jacob were all buried near the ancient site of Jerusalem. On the day Jesus was nailed to the Cross, we are told that tombs nearby opened, and many holy people arose in resurrection life and were seen walking about the city (Matthew 27:52-53). In faith, Jacob asked to be buried near the spot where the Messiah would be crucified. God honored that faith and raised many holy people to life in order to glimpse the city they had only dreamed of![26]

PRAYER

Our Father who is in heaven, what a kind heavenly Father you are, and how You care about our families!! You arranged for Jacob, after all those years to see his beloved son again! If You cared that much about their family, You also care about our families and desire our relationships to be healed and restored. You desire us to forgive one another and love one another even as Joseph forgave his brothers. In Jesus' Name. Amen.

DAY 34

JACOB'S PROPHETIC PROPHECIES

Let me prophesy to you about your future destinies.
—Genesis 49:1 TPT; READ ALSO Genesis 49-50

As the end drew near for Jacob, the Spirit of Prophecy fell upon him. He became a shaper of destiny for his children as God revealed to him the future of his sons and God's plan for each one. "The rest of the Old Testament and all the New Testament are the development of Genesis 49. These verses require the whole Bible for their understanding."[27] We will look at three of the tribes.

"Like a lion, ... the scepter of rulership will not be taken from Judah, nor the ruler's staff from his descendants, until the Shiloh comes and takes what is due him, for the obedience of nations belongs to him" (v. 9-10 TPT). Judah is a picture of the One who is seen as the Mighty Lion of Judah. Jesus is the One who places his all-powerful hand on the neck of his enemies and delivers us. The lion is the king of beasts and terrifies its prey with his loud roar. The lion is a conqueror. Jesus is the Lion of the Tribe of Judah.

"Zebulun will settle along the seashore and become a safe harbor for ships, and his borders will extend to Sidon" (v. 13 TPT). The people of Zebulun were the first to see this great Light dawning (Matthew 4:15-16). The disciples of Galilee were like a fleet of ships carrying the light of the gospel to the nations. It was from a mountaintop

in Galilee that Jesus sent out his disciples to the nations (Matthew 28:16-19).

"*Issachar is a strong donkey lying down between its saddlebags. When he sees that his resting place is good, and his portion is so pleasant, then he will bend his shoulder to the burden and labor for his master*" (v. 14-15 TPT). This tribe is made up of people who are meant to be burden bearers. These are those "*who had understanding of the times, to know what Israel ought to do*" (1 Chronicles 12:32). They are a picture of the intercessors who bear others' burdens and take these to the Lord in prayer. There is an anointing of rest for those who give their lives in intercession.

PRAYER

> *Father, give us a spirit of wisdom like You gave Jacob to be able to discern the destinies and callings of our children and pray and speak into them. Help us to see others' callings and speak into them as well. In Jesus' Name. Amen.*

EXODUS

DAY 35

WOMEN WHO FEARED GOD

> But the midwives feared God, and did not
> do as the king of Egypt commanded them,
> but saved the male children alive.
> —Exodus 1:17; READ ALSO Exodus 1-2

THE NAMES OF the two midwives who saved the babies were Shiphrah and Puah. "Their names mean something like 'beauty' and 'splendor' respectively."[28] Their names' meanings show how God sees those who truly fear Him and what He thinks of those who fear Him more than they fear what man or wicked leaders think. These brave women were more afraid of angering God by destroying innocent babies than they were afraid of disobeying Pharaoh.

This command of Pharaoh's to kill the male babies is consistent with the enemy's plan to thwart God's plan of birthing the Messiah, as the Messiah would come through Israel.

Jochebed, the mother of Moses, was also a woman mightily used of God. Jochebed saw when Moses was born that he was a beautiful child. Fearing and trusting God, she made an ark of bulrushes for him and laid it in the reeds by the river's bank. This was a courageous act and showed her trust that somehow God was going to take care of her child. She surrendered her most valuable possession into God's care.

As it turned out, Pharaoh's daughter found him and delivered him from death. Then she asked Jochebed to nurse him. This way Moses' mother was able to train him in the Hebrew heritage in his early years and be paid for it! It is ironic that Pharaoh's own daughter was raising a son, a Hebrew slave, who would end up delivering Israel out of the slavery in Egypt.

Jochebed not only saved her son but was used by God through devotion and diligence to preserve a nation.

PRAYER

> *Father in heaven, we are so thankful for the courageous women that were used to protect the nation that would bring forth the Seed of the woman—Jesus. Thank You that they feared, revered, and held in awe the King of Kings and Lord of Lords. Raise up brave women today who will value the lives of their children and raise them to be mighty for You. In Jesus' Name. Amen.*

Exodus

DAY 36

THE ANGEL OF THE LORD

> And the Angel of the LORD appeared to him in a flame of fire from the midst of a bush. So he looked, and behold, the bush was burning with fire, but the bush was not consumed.
> —Exodus 3:2; READ ALSO Exodus 3

There are unusual aspects of this "Angel." This "Angel" receives worship, although no angel can receive worship but God alone. The angel Lucifer was expelled from heaven for trying to receive such worship. The mystery is solved in this text as he is revealed to be the Lord God (see Acts 7:30-32). But how could Moses and other Old Testament persons have seen God face-to-face and lived, since Scripture clearly states the contrary (Exodus 33:20)? "The answer: because they saw the Jesus in a preincarnate form, known in the Old Testament as the Angel of the Lord—the Messenger of the covenant" (Malachi 3:1)[29].

This "Angel" appears in a flame of fire. This was an unusual phenomenon because the bush did not burn up. The burning bush is also a picture of the cross.

> The Hebrew word used to describe this bush comes from the word "to stick or to prick," this meaning a thorn-bush or bramble. We can think of the cross – where Jesus, crowned with thorns, endured the fires of judgment and yet was not consumed by them – and be reminded of the cross when we consider the burning bush.[30]

The fire of God is often used by God to give tangible evidence of His power, His presence, and His holiness. The "Angel" said, *"Take your sandals off your feet, for the place where you stand is holy ground"* (Exodus 3:6). God told Moses to tell the children of Israel that *"I AM"* has sent him to deliver them out of Egypt.

PRAYER

> *Our Father who is in heaven, it is so astonishing to see Your Son as "The Angel of the LORD", and as a type of the "burning bush." You planned ahead with the details of our salvation in having Moses live in the desert at Mount Sinai where the Ten Commandments were given. Give us eyes to see you in every book and chapter in the Old Testament. We worship You, Jesus, as our Savior and Lord. In Your Name, Amen.*

Exodus

DAY 37

WHAT DO YOU HAVE IN YOUR HAND?

> So the LORD said to him, "What is that in your hand?" He said, "A rod."
> —Exodus 4:2; READ ALSO Exodus 4-6

THE FIRST SIGN that God was going to use Moses to deliver his people from Egypt was the rod becoming a snake; when he reached out to catch it, it became a rod again. The next sign was when he put his hand in his bosom and it became leprous; when he put it back in, it was restored. The last sign was when he took water from the river and poured it on the dry land; the water then became blood.

God used what Moses had in his hand. He did not use the scepter that was in Moses' royal hand when he lived in Egypt, but He did use the simple shepherd's staff.

God likes to use what is in our hand. God used Shamgar's ox goad to kill six hundred men and deliver Israel (Judges 3:31). God used the stone in David's sling to kill Goliath and deliver Israel from the Philistines (1 Samuel 17:49). God used the jawbone of a donkey in Samson's hand (Judges 15:15). God used five loaves and two fish in the hand of a boy to feed five thousand (John 6:9).

God used the rod of Moses that would part the Red Sea. It would strike a rock and water would pour forth. It would be raised over the battle until Israel would win. It would be called *"the rod of God"* (Exodus 4:20 and 17:9).

We need to ask ourselves what we have in our hand. Do we have a cell phone so we can call and encourage someone? Can we speak? Can we sing? Can we play an instrument? Can we draw? Can we drive a vehicle? Can we cook? Can we pray and intercede? Can we visit a shut in? A widow? An orphan?

PRAYER

> *Our Father in heaven, help us to see what we "have in our hand" and use it for the kingdom of God. Lord, we dedicate our time, our talents, and our resources for Your purposes and Your glory!! Release creativity to us to see what we do have available and then strategies to use it in ways that please You. Help us to "think outside the box" for ways we can use what You have already given us. Help us to remember that we have the Creator inside of us and His ideas. In Jesus' Name. Amen.*

DAY 38

A HARD HEART

> But Pharaoh hardened his heart at this time also; neither would he let the people go.
> —Exodus 8:32; READ ALSO Exodus 7-8

THE PHARAOH AT the time of the Exodus was Amenhotep III. He was the head of the greatest nation known; his power was immense, and he was probably the richest king in the world. He had a huge force of slaves—the Israelites. Because of his great arrogance and pride, he was doomed.[31]

Pharaoh had hardened his own heart and said *"Who is the LORD, that I should obey His voice to let Israel go? I do not know the LORD, nor will I let Israel go"* (Exodus 5:2). Because of this, God would strengthen Pharaoh in the evil he already chose. Even as God hardened Pharaoh's heart, He also gave him reasons to believe and surrender to God – if he wanted to. God can do the same in our rebellion. *"God also gave them up to uncleanness, in the lusts of their hearts"* (Romans 1:24a).

God hardened Pharaoh's heart to bring righteous judgment upon Egypt, and in doing so would reveal Himself even to those who rejected Him. His miracles and judgments would be an invitation for the Egyptians to personally believe in the Lord.

When Pharaoh asked for a miracle, Aaron was instructed to cast down his rod. When he did, it became a great serpent or crocodile, which was a symbol of Egypt itself.[32] The magicians or sorcerers of Egypt were able to do this also. Miracles are also part of Satan's arsenal. (See 2 Thessalonians 2:9-10). The astonishing part of this miracle is that Aaron's rod swallowed up their rods. This showed God was bigger than their gods!

Each of the ten plagues was a judgment against the Egyptian gods. The first plague was the Nile becoming blood. They worshipped the Nile, and *Khnum,* the god who was to guard the Nile. This plague showed he was unable to protect his territory.

PRAYER

> *Father in heaven, You desire that we have a soft heart. You told us in Your Word that You would give us a new heart and put a new spirit within us; that You would take out our heart of stone and give us a heart of flesh (Ezekiel 36:26). We desire a pliable heart that loves You. Amen!*

DAY 39

LET MY PEOPLE GO

> Then Moses said, "Thus says the LORD: 'About midnight I will go out into the midst of Egypt; and all the firstborn in the land of Egypt shall die, from the firstborn of Pharaoh who sits on his throne, even to the firstborn of the female servant...'"
> —Exodus 11:4-5; READ ALSO Exodus 9-11

GOD SAID THAT after this last plague, there would be a great cry throughout the land of Egypt, such as was never heard before. But there would be peace in Goshen so that even the dogs would not bark. It would be seen in that day that God does make a distinction between the Egyptians and Israel, and that everyone would know that God makes a difference between those who know Him and those who do not.

Pharaoh would let the Israelites go. In fact, he would drive them out. Each Israelite was to ask from his neighbor articles of silver and articles of gold. The Egyptians were more than willing to give these gifts to persuade them to leave. This was how the slaves of Israel received their past wages from their time of slavery, and how they did not leave Egypt empty-handed.

> These jewels were employed afterwards in the adornment and enrichment of the Sanctuary. They flashed in the breastplate of the High Priest, and shone in the sacred vessels.[33]

The wonders of God were manifested in such a way through the ten plagues that the gods of Egypt were thoroughly defeated. One example is the ninth plague of darkness which was against Ra, the sun god. Pharaoh was believed to be the incarnation of the sun god. More than 400 years later, the Philistines remembered the LORD God of Israel as the one who plagued the Egyptians (1 Samuel 4:8).

PRAYER

> *Our Father who is in heaven, we praise you that you do make a distinction between those who are your people and those who are not. Just like you gave Moses and Aaron authority over the false gods of Egypt, you give us authority over the false gods of today. Let Your light shine in our darkness today! In Jesus' Name. Amen!*

DAY 40
THE PASSOVER

> For the LORD will pass through to strike the Egyptians; and when He sees the blood on the lintel and on the two doorposts, the LORD will pass over the door and not allow the destroyer to come into your houses to strike you.
> —Exodus 12:23; READ ALSO Exodus 12-13

Passover is the celebration of God's love and power in delivering His people out of the hand of their enemy.

After the death of the firstborn was announced as the last plague, God made a way of escape for the Israelites. They were to choose a lamb and kill it. The blood of the lamb was to be placed on the doorposts and lintel of the doorway, and when the death angel saw it, he was to pass over that house.

Passover is a celebration of Jesus. 1 Corinthians 5:7 says, *"For indeed Christ, our Passover, was sacrificed for us."* Think about what happened when the father applied the blood to the lintel. He dipped a branch of hyssop into the blood and applied the blood in the form of a cross. God accepted the death of that lamb in place of Israel's firstborn. The angel of death passed over them. God's deliverance ALWAYS comes by His cross and by His blood!

Many wonderful things happened at Passover:

- By the blood of the lamb, Israel was REDEEMED!
- The judgment of God was turned away from them!
- The gods of Egypt were judged: their power broken!
- Israel was released from oppression and bondage!
- They were set free to enter God's promise![34]

All the firstborn died at midnight from the firstborn of Pharaoh to the captive in the dungeon to the firstborn of livestock. King Tut who was to be Amenhotep IV, the firstborn of Pharaoh died. His brother Akhenaton took his place.[35] Imagine the cry!!

PRAYER

> *Father in heaven, we praise and thank You for the promise that we, too, are delivered by the Blood of the Lamb. When we by faith put the blood of Jesus over our doorpost, the death angel passes over us, and we are free from the deadly pestilence and all evil! In Jesus' Name. Amen!*

Exodus

DAY 41
THE RED SEA CROSSING

> And He took off their chariot wheels, so that they drove them with difficulty; and the Egyptians said, "Let us flee from the face of Israel, for the LORD fights for them against the Egyptians." Then the LORD said to Moses, "Stretch out your hand over the sea, that the waters may come back upon the Egyptians, on their chariots and on their horsemen."
> —Exodus 14:25-26; READ ALSO Exodus 14-15

This is the story of one of the greatest miracles of all time!! After Israel left Egypt, Pharaoh changed his mind and took six hundred choice chariots and all the chariots of Egypt with captains and pursued the Israelites. When they saw the Egyptians, they cried out to the Lord! Moses said, *"Do not be afraid. Stand still, and see the salvation of the Lord,...For the Egyptians whom you see today, you shall see again no more forever"* (v.13).

God told Moses to lift up his rod and stretch it out over the sea and divide it. He did and the children of Israel went over on dry ground!!! The Egyptians then followed them into the sea. When Moses stretched out his hand over the sea again, all the Egyptians drowned in the sea, including Pharoah.

Ron Wyatt, an archaeologist from the Nashville area went to explore where the Israelites crossed the Red Sea. The Israelites actually crossed the Sinai peninsula and crossed the Gulf of Aqaba over into Saudi Arabia; they did not cross at the Gulf of Suez.

When his team got to the beach of Nuweiba, across from Saudi Arabia, they dived into the Gulf and found coral encrusted chariot remains. The coral was the agent used to preserve the chariot remains. We read in Exodus 14:25 that angels took off the wheels of the chariots as they drove them in the midst of the sea. Ron found several six-spoked wheels as well as an eight-spoked wheel. In 1988, Ron found a four-spoked gold chariot wheel, which looked almost perfect. Experts in history say that the four, six and eight-spoked wheels were only used at the time of the Exodus.[36]

PRAYER

> *How amazing that these finds support the Bible in every detail!! If You delivered the Israelites from their enemies in such an astounding and miraculous way, nothing is too hard for You to help us also!! Amen!*

DAY 42

THE MIRACLE OF MANNA

> And the children of Israel ate manna forty years, ... until they came to the border of the land of Canaan.
> —Exodus 16:35 READ ALSO Exodus 16-18

WE CAN SEE Jesus in the many miracles of the Lord after the children of Israel left Egypt!! When Moses brought the children of Israel from the Red Sea, they went into the wilderness and there was no water. When they came to Marah, the water was bitter. The Lord showed him to throw a tree into it, and when he did, it became sweet. Jesus died on a tree, and when we turn our bitter situations over to Him, He heals them! He reveals Himself here as Jehovah-Rapha, the God who heals us.

In the Wilderness of Sin, the people complained because of no food. Then the Lord said to Moses, *"I will rain bread from heaven for you"* (Exodus 16:4). Jesus says in John 6:35: *"I am the bread of life. He who comes to Me shall never hunger, and he who believes in Me shall never thirst."* Jesus is the Manna from heaven.

In chapter 17, the children of Israel camped in Rephidim, but there was no water, so the complaining continued. The LORD told Moses to strike the rock, and when he did, water came out of it. Jesus said, *"...whoever drinks of the water that I shall give him will never thirst...it will become in him a fountain of water springing up into everlasting life"* (John 4:14).

It was also at Rephidim where the Amalekites were

defeated. Aaron and Hur supported Moses' hands and as they held them up, the Israelites won; when they let their hands down, they lost. Moses built an altar there and called it "Jehovah Nissi." Jesus is always our banner of victory in every battle. Just as Moses defeated the Amalekites, we will defeat all our enemies.

PRAYER

> *Jesus, You showed Yourself in so many ways to the Israelites as they came out of Egypt. You delivered them from their enemies, you provided manna in the wilderness. You brought them water out of the rock! Jesus, You taught us in the New Testament that You never change. You are the bread of life. You are living water and if we drink of this water, we'll never thirst again!! In Your Name. Amen.*

DAY 43

MOUNT SINAI

> Now Mount Sinai was completely in smoke, because the LORD descended upon it in fire. Its smoke ascended like the smoke of a furnace, and the whole mountain quaked greatly. And when the blast of the trumpet sounded long and became louder and louder, Moses spoke, and God answered him by voice.
> —Exodus 19:18-19; READ ALSO Exodus 19-20

These signs of power and glory signaled the presence of God. The whole environment spoke of God's presence in a terrifying sense. What Israel saw and felt in the thunder, lightning, the cloud, the smoke, and the earthquake was terrifying. However, the sound of the trumpet came from heaven itself. No wonder all the people trembled.

There is significant evidence that this took place in the Jebel el Lawz range in Saudi Arabia. As Ron Wyatt explored this area, one of the mountains in this range, Jebal Maqla was blackened as if it had been on fire.[37] In Galatians 4:25, Paul clearly says Mount Sinai was in Arabia.

This is the place where God gave the 10 commandments.

1. You shall have no other gods before Me.

2. You shall not make for yourself a carved image.

3. You shall not take the name of the LORD your God in vain.

4. Remember the Sabbath day, to keep it holy.

5. Honor your father and your mother, that your days may be long upon the land which the LORD your God is giving you.

6. You shall not murder.

7. You shall not commit adultery.

8. You shall not steal.

9. You shall not lie.

10. You shall not covet.

PRAYER

Father in heaven, we are so thankful for Your laws!! Our nation was based on these laws, and as we follow them, we can live in peace. Help us as a nation to honor these ten commandments and repent where we have broken them!!! Jesus, you said that if we loved the Lord with all our hearts and loved our neighbor as ourselves, we would fulfill the Law and the Prophets. Amen!!

DAY 44

RESTITUTION

> If a man steals an ox or a sheep, and slaughters it or sells it, he shall restore five oxen for an ox and four sheep for a sheep.
> —Exodus 22:1; READ ALSO Exodus 21-22

THE MOSAIC LAW did not require a man to go to jail for theft. Instead, he was required to restore what he stole, plus add an additional penalty. In this passage, the penalty could be anywhere from 500% (restoring five oxen for an ox) to 400% (restoring four sheep for a sheep), to restoring double.

Restitution applies to us today. It is not enough to say, "I'm sorry." Restitution restores trust. It brings healing to hearts that have been betrayed, wounded, or broken.

In Luke 19:1-10, we read the story of Zacchaeus. When he repented of his sins, he said to Jesus, *"Look, Lord! Here and now I give half of my possessions to the poor, and if I have cheated anybody out of anything, I will pay back four times the amount."* Jesus said, *"Today salvation has come to this house...."* (v. 8) NIV

> Zacchaeus recognized that these people he had stolen from were sheep, so he was willing to pay back four times the amount he had stolen. Jesus commended Zacchaeus for this. He told him that because of his actions, he was saved and recognized that he was a son of Abraham. Jesus then said that He had come to seek and to save what was lost.

For the one who has been stolen from, restitution helps him to forgive. It restores trust and love. For the offender, restitution enables him to feel the pain he has caused others. It writes on his heart the price of his actions.[38] Restitution is a necessary part of repentance.

PRAYER

Lord, we repent for the sins we have committed, and we are very sorry for the way we have treated others. Please show us ways that we can do restitution and help restore trust in relationships that have been broken! Write on our hearts the pain we have caused others. Thank You for Your healing and restoring power. Thank You that because of Your sacrifice, we have peace through the blood of Your cross (Colossians 1:20). In Jesus' Name. Amen.

DAY 45

MY NAME IS IN THE ANGEL

> Behold, I send an Angel before you to keep you in the way and to bring you into the place which I have prepared. Beware of Him and obey His voice; do not provoke Him, for He will not pardon your transgressions; for My name is in Him.
> —Exodus 23:20-21; read also Exodus 23-24

This is a unique angel who commanded obedience from Israel and had the right of judgment over the nation. The name of God was in this angel!

This is another Old Testament appearance of none other than Jesus before His incarnation in Bethlehem. This Angel often speaks directly as the Lord.

The name Yahweh is in Jesus. His name is literally *Yahshua*. Jesus was with Israel in all their wilderness experiences. "This Angel with the authority and prestige of the name of God was evidence enough that God himself was present in his Son."[39]

This same principle is true in our lives with Jesus today. He not only goes before us to prepare a place for us in heaven (John 14:2-3), but He directs our steps today and each day as we look to Him.

As we walk obediently with Him, He gives us the following wonderful promises: "*So you shall serve the LORD your God, and He will bless your bread and your water. And I will take sickness away from the midst of you. No one shall suffer miscarriage or be barren in your land; I will fulfill the number of your days"* (Exodus 23:25-26).

PRAYER

Thank You Yeshua that you indeed guide and direct our steps each day. We want to love and obey you. And You have promised us in Ephesians 1:3 that You have blessed us with every spiritual blessing in the heavenly places in Christ. One of the most life-giving blessings is that You will take away sickness from us, and we will not be barren or have miscarriages. We will fulfill our destiny and You will give us a full life span!! In Jesus' Name. Amen.

DAY 46

THE TABERNACLE

> And let them make Me a sanctuary (tabernacle), that I may dwell among them.
> —Exodus 25:8; read also Exodus 25-26

THE TABERNACLE IS a type and shadow of Jesus Christ. It was built after the pattern of the heavenly Tabernacle, and it is symbolic of Jesus' death on the Cross, His atoning blood that was shed at Calvary, and His role as mediator between God and man. It also foretold of the day when God would send the Holy Spirit to indwell, or "tabernacle" with man. The Tabernacle was shaped like a cross. The placement of the furniture, as well as the tribes that encamped around it, formed a cross which pointed all those who saw it to Jesus Christ, the mediator between God and man.

The Tabernacle was divided into three parts: the outer court, the holy place, and the Most Holy Place.

The altar of burnt offering was the first piece seen after entering in at the east gate in the outer court. Next was the bronze laver. Inside the holy place was the gold lampstand on the south side, the table of showbread on the north side, and the altar of incense before the veil. The Most Holy Place was behind the veil and contained the ark of the covenant.

The Ark of the Covenant was located in the Holy of Holies. It was made of wood and covered with gold. It contained the golden pot of manna, Aaron's rod, and the Ten

Commandments. Jesus is our Ark of the Covenant—the fulfillment of the law for us.

The mercy seat was made of pure gold with two cherubim of gold at the two ends of the mercy seat. Their wings were stretched out over the mercy seat as they faced each other. The mercy seat was placed on the top of the ark of the covenant. The high priest went into the Holy of Holies once a year to sprinkle blood on the mercy seat on the Day of Atonement. The blood cried for mercy, and it was there that Jesus took His blood after His resurrection for the forgiveness of our sins (Hebrews 9:11-15).

PRAYER

Jesus, thank You for all the Old Testament pictures of Your sacrifice in the New Testament!! Thank You for shedding Your blood for us! Amen.

Exodus

DAY 47

THE BRONZE ALTAR

> You shall make an altar of acacia wood...
> and you shall overlay it with bronze.
> —EXODUS 27:1A, 2C; READ ALSO EXODUS 27-28

THE BRONZE ALTAR was the first piece of furniture the Israelites saw when they entered the outer court. This brass (bronze) altar was a picture of judgment for sin.

The altar became the most important piece of furniture because sacrifices were made on it. Everything in the Tabernacle was somehow connected to the bronze altar. The blood from the altar was sprinkled upon the mercy seat, and the fire from the altar was used to light the golden candlestick. Even the fire for the altar of incense and the meal for the loaves of showbread had some part in the bronze altar. When the children of Israel entered the outer court with their burnt offering, they were saying to God, "I am consecrating myself and my substance to You."

The bronze altar points to Jesus who is the sacrifice for our sins. In offering Himself on the Cross, Jesus consecrated Himself to God to do His will. Jesus died for our sins.

The bronze altar was made from mirrors. Imagine the priests seeing a reflection of themselves in the polished bronze surface of the altar. "Watching an animal shedding its blood and burning on the altar directly above your own image in the bronze plate of that altar, would leave a strong impression in your memory of the cost of the atonement for your sin."[40]

Any discussion of the bronze altar must include not only Christ's death for us but also our death to self. We cannot go into the Holy of Holies until we have made the choice to sacrifice ourselves. We do this as we: a) recognize all known sin and confess it, b) release others through forgiveness, and c) receive His forgiveness.[41]

Paul said, *"I die daily"* (1 Corinthians 15:31).

PRAYER

> *We give praise to You Father that when we approach Your throne today, that You do not see our unholiness or unrighteousness. Instead, You see our right standing with You through Jesus shed blood on the cross. Amen!*

Exodus

DAY 48

THE ALTAR OF INCENSE

> You shall make an altar to burn incense on; you shall make it of acacia wood.... And you shall put it before the veil that is before the ark of the Testimony, before the mercy seat that is over the Testimony, where I will meet with you.
> —Exodus 30:1,6; read also Exodus 29-30

THE GOLDEN ALTAR of incense foreshadowed Jesus, our High Priest, Who makes intercession to the Father on our behalf and Who presents our praises to the Father.

There were two altars in the Tabernacle—the bronze altar in the outer court where the animals were sacrificed, and the altar of incense in the Holy Place where a different kind of sacrifice was made—prayer.

Fire from the brazen altar was used to burn the incense. The priest took some of the coals of fire from the bronze altar and would put them in a cup where they burned incense on the altar. They could not bring just any coals to burn the incense because it could cost them their lives. Aaron's two sons were an example of this. One day they decided to offer up "strange fire" unto God, and the fire of the Lord consumed them (Leviticus 10:1,2).

The incense burned on the altar is symbolic of prayer. Incense is described as sweet, pure, holy, and perpetual. This describes Jesus' prayer for us. Jesus is right now at the right hand of God interceding for us (Romans 8:34). Jesus presents our praises to the Father as well. By Him, we offer the sacrifice of praise to God continually (Hebrews 13:15).

The real golden altar in heaven appears in Revelation 8:1-5. We can see from these verses that incense is all about the prayer of the Church. Our prayers are filling up the bowls in heaven. When these bowls are filled, they are combined with incense, and then they are released as answers from heaven.

PRAYER

> *Father, we are so privileged to join with Your Son Jesus Who is always interceding for us at Your right hand. This intercession is our highest calling, for it is the calling of Jesus Himself. Teach us how to pray in the power of the Holy Spirit and pray to the Father in the name of Jesus as You instructed us in John 16:24. In Your name we pray. Amen.*

DAY 49

THE GOLDEN CALF

> And I said to them, 'Whoever has any gold, let them break it off'. So they gave it to me, and I cast it into the fire, and this calf came out.
> —Exodus 32:23; read also Exodus 31-33

After Moses had been on the mountain of the Lord for forty days, the children of Israel went to Aaron and asked him to make gods for them. How we handle delays is a good measure of our spiritual maturity.

Aaron told the people to bring their gold earrings to him. He melted them down and fashioned them into a gold calf or bull. The people proclaimed it as their god that brought them out of Egypt. The statue of the calf did not exist the day before, but now they worshipped it as though it had brought them out of Egypt!

God wanted to destroy the nation, but Moses interceded and asked the Lord what the other nations would say. Would they say that God could bring them out of Egypt, but not into the promised land which He had promised to their ancestors? God relented.

When Moses saw the people dancing and worshipping the calf, he threw the stone tablets (10 Commandments) to the ground. He melted the calf they had made, ground it into powder, mixed it with water, and made the people drink it. Then he asked the Lord to forgive them for this great sin.

The Lord told Moses to lead them into the land He

promised Abraham, Isaac, and Jacob. Moses asked who the LORD would send with him to help him, and He said He would go with him.

Moses asked to see God's glory. The LORD said He would make all His goodness pass before him, but he would not be able to look directly at His face for no one could see His face and live.

What is God's glory? His goodness. God is <u>completely</u> good. There is no evil in Him at all!! He is perfect in love and mercy!!

PRAYER

> *Our Father, like Moses we desire to see Your glory. You said You would reveal Your goodness to us!! Your goodness is revealed in Your forgiving our sins, healing our bodies, healing our broken hearts, and healing our broken relationships. We give You praise today for Your goodness. Your love and mercy endure forever!! Thank You Jesus! Amen.*

Exodus

DAY 50

THE FEAST OF HARVEST

> Three times in the year all your men shall appear before the Lord, the Lord God of Israel.
> —Exodus 34:23; read also Exodus 34-35

Moses cut two more tablets of stone, and the LORD wrote again the 10 Commandments. God then renewed the covenant that He would bring them into the promised land and drive out the inhabitants, but they were to destroy all the remains of their idolatry. They were not to make covenant with or marry these people.

They were told to keep Passover and the Feast of Unleavened Bread in the month of Abib, the Feast of Weeks (Pentecost) and the Feast of Ingathering (Tabernacles). Three times they were to appear before the Lord.

Pentecost was the festival that occurred fifty days after Passover. It is called the Feast of Weeks and also the Feast of Harvest, because it was on that day that the Jewish people presented to the Lord the firstfruits of the annual wheat harvest.

We learn in Acts 2, that when the Day of Pentecost had fully come, that the Holy Spirit was poured out and they all spoke with other tongues. They received power from on high to be witnesses in Jerusalem, Judea, Samaria and to the uttermost parts of the earth. This was precisely the day when the Jews were to lift their hands to the Lord and give thanks for the harvest.

The disciples were about to begin reaping a harvest of

souls that has continued now for almost 2,000 years. Jesus said, *"The harvest truly is plentiful, but the laborers are few. Therefore, pray the Lord of the harvest to send out laborers into His harvest"* (Matthew 9: 37,38).

The disciples in the upper room were praying the power of the Holy Spirit would come upon them to carry the gospel to all the earth. They were praying to be laborers in the harvest field.

PRAYER

> *Father in heaven, what an awesome plan you had to bring the Israelites back to their promised land. Even as they were leaving Egypt, You had plans for Jesus to send His Holy Spirit, and send Your people back into the harvest fields to tell them about Jesus, and save all nations. Amen!*

Exodus

DAY 51

SEEING JESUS IN THE TABERNACLE FURNITURE

And Bezalel and Aholiab, and every gifted artisan in whom the Lord has put wisdom and understanding,... shall do according to all that the Lord has commanded.
—EXODUS 36:1; READ ALSO EXODUS 36-38

As THE ISRAELITES entered the Outer Court, the first piece of furniture was the Bronze Altar, which is where the animal sacrifices were made. This points to Jesus as the sacrifice for our sins. *"Who does not need daily, as those high priests, to offer up sacrifices, first for His own sins, and then for the people's: for this He did once for all when He offered up Himself"* (Hebrews 7:27).

The next piece of furniture was the Bronze Laver. This is where the priests would come for cleansing. They must be pure to enter the presence of God. Jesus cleanses us from our sins. *"That He might sanctify and cleanse her with the washing of water by the word"* (Ephesians 5:26).

Moving into the Holy Place, the Table of Showbread was on the north side. There were twelve loaves, one for every tribe. Jesus is the Bread of Life. *"I am the living bread which came down from heaven. If anyone eats of this bread, he will live forever; ..."* (John 6:51).

On the south side of the Holy Place was the Golden Lampstand; its purpose was to provide light in the Holy Place. This points to Jesus who is the light of the world, "*the true Light which gives light to every man coming into the world*" (John 1:9).

On the west side of the Holy Place in front of the veil was the Golden Altar of Incense where the priests prayed for the people. This altar points to Jesus who makes intercession for us.

The Ark of the Covenant was behind the veil in the Holy of Holies. It contained the 10 Commandments, Aaron's rod that budded, and the golden pot of manna. On the top was the mercy seat with the two cherubim. The high priest sprinkled blood on the mercy seat once a year. Jesus sprinkled His blood on the mercy seat for the remission of our sins. He is our Ark.

PRAYER

> *Jesus, we see You in every piece of furniture in the tabernacle. We will not miss this amazing prophetic picture of the Son of God! Amen.*

Exodus

DAY 52
THE CLOUD AND THE GLORY

> Then the cloud covered the tabernacle of meeting, and the glory of the Lord filled the tabernacle. And Moses was not able to enter the tabernacle of meeting, because the cloud rested above it, and the glory of the Lord filled the tabernacle.
> —Exodus 40:34-35; read also Exodus 38-40

THERE ARE SEVERAL examples in the Old Testament where the glory of God filled the tabernacle or temple, and the people could not even enter it because of the glory cloud filling the place. This was a notable sign of their love and obedience to follow His directions.

The same thing happened when Solomon completed and dedicated the temple – the glory of God so filled the temple they could not continue ministering there (1 Kings 8:10-11).

Without the glory, it was just a fancy tent. The same could be said of a church, of a home or of the human tent.

Smith Wigglesworth is an example of God's glory filling a human tent. Once when he was traveling to Cardiff in South Wales, he had been much in prayer on the journey. The carriage was full of people whom he knew to be unsaved, but there was so much talking and joking he could not get a word in for Jesus. As the train was nearing the station, he went to wash his hands so as to be ready to head straight to the meeting. As he returned to the carriage, a man jumped up and said, "Sir, you convince me of sin," and fell on his knees there and then. Soon the whole carriage of people were crying out the same way. They said, "Who are you? What are you? You convince us all of sin." Smith made the best of it, and many were born into the kingdom of God in that railway carriage.[42]

When the glory of God moves in, people are convicted of sin. They are healed of all manner of sickness and disease. Jesus is the same yesterday, today, and forever!

PRAYER

> *Our Father in heaven, how we long for Your glory to fill our lives, our churches, our cities, and our nation! How we long for Your glory and presence to so fill us so that wherever we go, lives are changed and brought into your kingdom. Your manifest presence leads to the most amazing healings. Let us live holy lives that are filled with the glory of God!! In Jesus' Name. Amen!*

LEVITICUS

DAY 53

SEEING JESUS IN THE SACRIFICES

> It is a burnt sacrifice, an offering made by fire, a sweet aroma to the Lord.
> —Leviticus 1:17b; read also Leviticus 1-2

THE FIVE OFFERINGS that were offered in the Tabernacle were important because they symbolized the provisions Jesus made for us when He offered His body as a sacrifice on the cross. The first offering the Israelites made was the burnt offering. The people were consecrating themselves and their substance to God.

The burnt offering was offered from the cattle, from the flocks—of the sheep or goats, or from the birds (Leviticus 1).

In offering Himself on the Cross Jesus consecrated Himself to God to do His will, and to us to become the sacrifice for our sins. He said, "I don't have to go to the cross, but I will. Not my will, but Yours be done."

The burnt offering points to the way the blood consecrates and dedicates us to God. The blood of the sacrifice was sprinkled on the altar to make atonement for the person sacrificing it.

The meal offering had to do with consecration of

possessions (Leviticus 2). We see that the composition of this offering consisted of flour, without leaven, oil, salt, and frankincense.

The flour refers to the perfect humanity of Christ (Hebrews 4:15). Leaven is a reference to sin in the Bible. No leaven was to be found, nor any impurity in this offering (1 Corinthians 5:7,8). This describes the sinless humanity of Jesus. Oil is a picture of the Holy Spirit. Frankincense was a sweet-smelling sacrifice as Jesus was (Ephesians 5:2). Salt was a preservative. Jesus' words brought preservation to all who heard and accepted them.

PRAYER

> *Our Father, we desire to consecrate ourselves and all we are and have to you today. We give of our substance to you and believe You will prosper us as it is written, "...that though He was rich, yet for your sakes He became poor, that you through His poverty might become rich" (2 Corinthians 8:9). We really desire that our lives might be a sweet- smelling sacrifice to You. May we spread the fragrance of Your presence everywhere we go!! In Jesus' Name. Amen.*

DAY 54

SEEING JESUS IN THE SACRIFICES (PART 2)

> When his offering is a sacrifice of a peace offering...whether male or female, he shall offer it without blemish before the Lord.
> —LEVITICUS 3:1; READ ALSO LEVITICUS 3-5

THE PEACE OFFERING (Leviticus 3) was a form of celebration for the Israelites and included the entire family and their friends. They would bring an animal and sacrifice it and the priest would sprinkle the blood all around the altar.

Jesus is our peace; we have peace through His blood. *"But now in Christ Jesus you who once were far off have been brought near by the blood of Christ. For He Himself is our peace, who has made both one, and has broken down the middle wall of separation"* (Ephesians 2:13-14). Your peace passes all understanding.

The sin and trespass offerings were two of the most important offerings. They dealt with transgressions and sin against God and others. The word sin means to "miss the mark." The sin offering was made when the Israelites had blown it with God. Through the blood of their animal sacrifices, their sins were atoned for, and they were once again in right standing with God.

The sin offering (Leviticus 4) represents forgiveness for the sins we commit against God. One of the first declarations about Jesus was that, "...*you shall call his name JESUS: for He will save His people from their sins*" (Matthew 1:21).

The trespass offering (Leviticus 5) was to remove the guilt of sin when man trespassed against man. Transgress means to go over the mark. This was made when the Israelites had hurt someone or trespassed against them. Jesus made a way for us to be reconciled to one another. *"And be kind to one another, tenderhearted, forgiving one another, even as God in Christ forgave you"* (Ephesians 4:32).

PRAYER

> *Jesus, You are our peace offering!! What a beautiful picture this peace offering is of You! You have reconciled all things to Yourself, whether things in heaven or things on earth, having made peace through the blood of Your cross. You are our peace!! You have broken down every wall between us and You, and between every person. In Jesus' Name. Amen.*

Leviticus

DAY 55

THE FIRE ON THE ALTAR SHALL NOT GO OUT

> A fire shall always be burning on the altar; it shall never go out.
> —LEVITICUS 6:13; READ ALSO LEVITICUS 6-7

THIS IS THE verse that Count von Zinzendorf received from the Holy Spirit in 1727 which inspired the Moravian's incredible 100-year prayer vigil, which was launched that year. He knew this was not only referring to the altar of sacrifice, but that it signified the prayer of the saints to restore unceasing prayer before the Lord. Church history, and therefore world history, would never be the same again.

The power of their persistent prayer produced a divine passion and zeal for missionary outreach to the lost. Many of them even sold themselves into slavery in places like Suriname in South America just so they could carry the light of the gospel into closed societies. The Moravians were the first missionaries to the slaves of St. Thomas in the Virgin Islands; they also went to strange places called Lapland and Greenland and to many places in Africa.[43]

They left on ships waving good-bye to parents they would never see again saying: "Don't cry for us. We are going to reap the rewards of the suffering of the Lamb!"

They wove their lives around "three strands." First, they had relational unity. Second, their prayer produced a divine passion for missionary outreach. Third, they had a motto that they lived by: "No one works unless someone prays." This led them to take two-hour vigils around the clock, day and night praying for others.

The Moravian group was known as "Herrnhut," and was located in southeastern Germany. Their 100-year prayer vigil and global missionary exploits marked one of the purest moves of the Spirit in church history and touched virtually every great missionary endeavor of the eighteenth and nineteenth century. One group won John Wesley to the Lord as he saw their peace in the midst of a great storm on a ship going to America.

PRAYER

> *Lord, let Your fire fall on us as it did the Moravians. Let us again begin unbroken prayer 24/7. May Your fire fall again so that the harvest fields of the world will be reached with the same passion and zeal!! Amen!*

Leviticus

DAY 56

THE GLORY FIRE AND THE PROFANE FIRE

> And fire came out from before the Lord and consumed the burnt offering and the fat on the altar. When all the people saw it, they shouted and fell on their faces.
> —Leviticus 9:24; read also Leviticus 8-10

AFTER THE SACRIFICIAL system had been instituted, Aaron now for the first time entered the tabernacle. After Aaron and Moses came out and blessed the people, the glory of the LORD appeared to all the people, and God proved His presence by sending the fire to light the sacrifice. This was obviously God's fire!

Fire is often associated with God's presence and work. In Deuteronomy 4:24 it says, *"the LORD your God is a consuming fire, a jealous God."* John the Baptist promised that Jesus would come with a baptism of the Holy Spirit and with fire (Matthew 3:11). The Holy Spirit manifested His presence on the day of Pentecost by tongues of fire (Acts 2:3).

Then Nadab and Abihu, the sons of Aaron each took his censer and put fire in it. This fire was profane fire in that it was a fire not kindled from the altar of burnt offering which was started by God Himself. It was fire not associated with the atoning and redeeming work of sacrifice. Perhaps in going "before the LORD," they may have dared to go past the veil into the Holy of Holies. So, fire went out from the LORD, and they died before the LORD. The same fire that showed forth God's glory now showed His judgment on these unfaithful priests[44] (Leviticus 10:2).

A modern-day example of the fire of God happened at the Azusa Street revival in 1906. As the people prayed in the Spirit, a literal fire would come out of the roof of the building; a fire about 50 feet away from it would come down and mingle with it. People would literally call the fire department because the building looked like it was burning![45] Send Your glory fire again, Lord!!

PRAYER

> *Lord, we see that even though Aaron's sons had seen firsthand all the miracles in bringing the nation out of Egypt and heard the voice of God and saw the fire, lightning, smoke, and felt the thunder and the earthquake with the rest of the nation at Mount Sinai, they still disobeyed God. Help us to always fear You and make Your Word our final authority! Amen.*

DAY 57

THE RITUAL AFTER CHILDBIRTH

> And if she is not able to bring a lamb, then she may bring two turtledoves or two young pigeons—one as a burnt offering and one as a sin offering.
> —LEVITICUS 12:8A; READ ALSO LEVITICUS 11-12

MOSES TOLD THE children of Israel that if a woman has conceived and given birth to a male child, she shall be unclean seven days. On the eighth day the child shall be circumcised.

Mary, the mother of Jesus, brought Him to the temple on the eighth day after His birth (Luke 2:21). Jesus obeyed the law in every respect, including His circumcision on the eighth day.

God commanded Abraham that his male covenant descendants should be circumcised when eight days old (Genesis 17:12). This was the sign of the covenant God made with Abraham and his covenant descendants (Genesis 17:11).

Circumcision is a cutting away of the flesh and a covenant sign for those that they should put no trust in the flesh. Also, because circumcision deals with the organ of procreation, it was a reminder of the special seed of Abraham, which would ultimately bring the Messiah.

The mother was to continue in the blood of her purification thirty-three days. Mary, the mother of Jesus, also fulfilled these days of purification (Luke 2:22-24). Every mother needed to go through this cleansing and then bring a lamb, or if they were too poor, they were to bring two turtledoves or two young pigeons. Jesus' family offered only a pair of turtledoves (Luke 2:22-24) at birth, showing they were not a wealthy family. After this, the mother was regarded as clean.

What a glimpse into Jesus' humiliation. He owned the cattle on a thousand hills, yet his parents were compelled to bring the poorest offering the law allowed. He became poor that we might become rich!

PRAYER

> *Lord, we see from the beginning how precious each child is, and what an amazing gift from God children are!! You said in Psalm 127: 3-5, "Behold, children are a heritage from the LORD, the fruit of the womb is a reward...Happy is the man who has his quiver full of them..." Praise Jesus!*

Leviticus

DAY 58

THE RITUAL FOR CLEANSING HEALED LEPERS

> And the priest shall go out of the camp, and the priest shall examine him; and indeed, if the leprosy is healed in the leper, then the priest shall command to take for him who is to be cleansed two living and clean birds, cedar wood, scarlet, and hyssop.
> —Leviticus 14:3-4; read also Leviticus 13-15.

WHAT A PICTURE of Jesus we have in these verses. After the person being cleansed of leprosy takes the two birds, one of them is to be killed in an earthen vessel over running water.

The living bird shall be taken with the cedar wood, the scarlet and the hyssop and shall be dipped in the blood of the bird that was killed over the running water. After this, the priest shall sprinkle the blood on the one cleansed from the leprosy seven times, and then the living bird is let loose in the open field.

This ritual can be summarized with these points:[46]

- This happened outside the camp. Jesus was sacrificed outside the camp (Hebrews 13:11-13).

- A thing of the heavens (bird) was sacrificed in an earthen vessel. Jesus was the Man from heaven (John 3:13, 6:38).

- This death, associated with water and blood, was applied to the leper, and applied perfectly (seven times) in connection with a living bird. Jesus came by water and blood (1 John 5:6) and died in association with water and blood (John 19:34-35).

- The sacrificial blood was also applied to scarlet yarn and a piece of wood, together with hyssop. Jesus died in association with scarlet cloth (Matthew 27:28), and with wood (John 19:17-18), and with hyssop (John 19:29).

- Bearing the mark of sacrifice, the living bird flew away, out of sight. Jesus ascended to heaven, out of sight.

PRAYER

Father in heaven, who could miss the striking resemblance of the cleansing of the leper, and the cleansing of our sins by our Savior. Every part of the picture is relevant and precise! Thank You for Jesus and for showing the details of His purpose in this passage. In Jesus' Name. Amen.

Leviticus

DAY 59

THE DAY OF ATONEMENT

> The goat will carry on itself all their sins to a solitary place; and the man shall release it in the desert.
> —LEVITICUS 16:22 NIV; READ ALSO LEVITICUS 16.

THE HIGH PRIEST did four things on the day of Atonement, requiring one ram, a bull and two goats.

He took the bull from the people, killed it and offered it as a sin offering for himself and his household. Aaron was to do this by himself. The tabernacle normally was a very busy place, with many priests and Levites and those bringing their offerings. But on this day the tabernacle was empty, except for one man doing his work. This was a preview of the perfect work of atonement to be made by Jesus the Messiah. There was no one with our Lord. He alone *"bore our sins in His own body on the tree, that we, having died to sins, might live for righteousness* (1 Peter 2:24).

He took the blood of that bull, with burning coals and incense, into the Holy of Holies behind the veil. He would burn the incense on the fire pan in the Most Holy Place, creating a cloud to cover the mercy seat. Then he sprinkled the blood on the mercy seat and in front of the mercy seat seven times.

The goat that was sacrificed was like Jesus in that the goat was spotless, was from the people of Israel, and was chosen by God. The goat's blood was taken to the Holy

Place to provide atonement for the people. Jesus provided atonement for our sins.

The other goat was called the "scapegoat." They confessed all the nation's sins on this goat, and it was released into the wilderness as a sign that the sins of the nation were taken away. This is a picture of Jesus in that He took all of our sins away. Jesus not only died for our sins, but He carried them away!!!

The Day of Atonement was completed by the sacrifice of the remaining ram.

PRAYER

> *We praise You Father for this amazing picture of the redemptive work of Christ. Jesus, you were put to death on the cross for our sin, like the first goat was killed. Then, like the second goat, you took all our sins and carried them away!! As far as the east is from the west, so far have You removed our transgressions from us!! (Psalm 103:12). Hallelujah! Amen.*

Leviticus

DAY 60
THE LAWS OF MORALITY

> You shall not lie with a male as with a woman. It is an abomination.
> —Leviticus 18:22 NIV; read also Leviticus 17-18

THE BIBLE IS very clear about what defiles the land: sexual sin (Leviticus 18:6-25), bloodshed and idolatry (Ezekiel 36:18), occult practices (Deuteronomy 18:10-12), and covenant breaking. The Bible even says the land will vomit out its inhabitants because of these sins (Leviticus 18:25).

The Bible calls homosexuality an abomination in verse 22 above. See also Jude 7. And yet in June 2015, the Supreme Court legalized gay marriage in Obergefell v. Hodges. Sadly, that night, the White House was lit with the colors of the rainbow.

Since that day the LGBT agenda has flourished. Our teenagers are taking hormones and having surgeries to make themselves a different sex. They do not realize that their heavenly Father created them with the gender they are for His purposes, and that we are to praise Him because we are fearfully and wonderfully made (Psalm 139:14).

We also have had many court cases where bakers, photographers, and other businesses were sued for not being willing to endorse gay marriages. As a result, they were forced into bankruptcy. (e.g., Melissa's Sweet Cakes, 2013).

Jesus said it would be like this in the last days where

sin would abound *and "evil men and impostors will grow worse and worse, deceiving and being deceived"* (2 Timothy 3:13).

Leviticus 18:21 states that *"you shall not let any of your descendants pass through the fire to Molech, nor shall you profane the name of your God: I am the LORD."* However, in 1973 we passed Roe vs. Wade and legalized abortion. We have the blood of over 60 million babies that have been aborted on our hands. Roe vs. Wade was overturned June 24, 2022!!

PRAYER

> *Lord, as we see the Day of the Lord approaching, we pray that we will humble ourselves and pray and seek Your face and turn from our wicked ways. Then You said You would forgive our sins and heal our land. We pray for a great revival and healing of our nation! In His Name. Amen.*

DAY 61

THE LAWS OF COMPASSION

You shall love your neighbor as yourself; I am the LORD.
—LEVITICUS 19:18B; READ ALSO LEVITICUS 19-20.

THIS CHAPTER BEGINS with *"You shall be holy, for I the LORD your God am holy."* The Hebrew word for holy is *qadosh* and means to set apart, dedicated to sacred purposes; holy, sacred, clean, morally or ceremonially pure. To be holy means to be more like God and separating ourselves from things that are not like Him and not according to His truth.

We can see Jesus' teachings coming straight from Leviticus. The law says that we are to honor our mother and father and keep the Sabbath (Leviticus 19:3). Keeping the Sabbath is found in the fourth commandment. Here we see submitting to parental authority is a step to submitting to Divine authority.[47]

The people were taught to not reap the corners of the fields but leave them to the poor, as well as the grapes on the vine. This was a wonderful way to provide for the poor. Jesus wanted "the least of these" taken care of. He said, *"And the King will answer and say to them, 'assuredly, I say to you, inasmuch as you did it to one of the least of these My brethren, you did it to Me'"* (Matthew 25:40).

Verse 18 was a center of Jesus' teachings. *"You shall not take vengeance, nor bear any grudge against the children of your people, but you shall love your neighbor as yourself: I am the LORD."* It is easy to cherish a grudge against another, but we must forgive everyone and love our neighbors and even our enemies. Both Jesus and Paul both cited this verse as a summary of the duties one has to his fellow man (Matthew 22:39-40, Romans 13:9).

Leviticus 19:28 admonished us to *"not make any cuttings in our flesh for the dead, nor tattoo any marks on our body."* This was imitating pagan customs, to worship devils or idols, and not fitting for the Lord's people. We are to be a holy people.

PRAYER

> *Lord, as we see Your day approaching, help us to be sanctified and set apart from society. But help us also to be salt and light in the world!! In Jesus' Name. Amen.*

Leviticus

DAY 62

SEEING JESUS IN THE SEVEN FEASTS

> Speak to the children of Israel and say to them: "The feasts of the Lord, which you shall proclaim to be holy convocations, these are My feasts."
> —Leviticus 23:2; read also Leviticus 21-23

Passover begins the biblical calendar. Passover is really a cluster of three closely related feasts: Passover, Unleavened Bread, and Firstfruits.

We discussed in our Day 40 devotional the Passover feast. It was a celebration of God delivering Israel out of Egypt. They put the blood of the lamb over the doorpost so the death angel would pass over them. This is symbolic of the blood of Jesus delivering us from the hand of our enemy.

The second feast is the Feast of Unleavened Bread (Leviticus 23:6-8). For the first Passover, the unleavened bread was a practical necessity because they left Egypt in such a hurry there was no time to allow for the bread dough to ferment with leaven (yeast) and rise. Spiritually speaking, this feast (and Jesus), was an illustration of the purity God wanted Israel to live out after Passover. Leaven is a picture of sin and corruption because a little leaven influences the whole lump of bread.

The third feast is the Feast of Firstfruits. Jesus was raised from the dead on Firstfruits. The children of Israel were to bring a sheaf of the first fruits of their harvest (barley) to the priest and he would wave it. It was a celebration of provision!

Pentecost was a celebration of God's blessings in three areas: a) His provision of harvest; b) His provision of the Word which was given on Mount Sinai; and c) God's provision of the Holy Spirit, which was given on Pentecost!

Church history shows that the church continued to observe these feasts for hundreds of years, even after they were outlawed by the Roman Emperor Constantine.

PRAYER

> *Lord, we love to celebrate what You celebrate. Our Passover Lamb has been sacrificed. You said, "Let us celebrate the Festival" (1 Corinthians 5:7-8 NLT). We rejoice in Your provision for us!!! In Jesus' name. Amen.*

Leviticus

DAY 63

SEEING JESUS IN THE SEVEN FEASTS - PART 2

> On the first day of the seventh month you are to have a day of rest, a sacred assembly commemorated with trumpet blasts... The tenth day is the Day of Atonement... On the fifteenth day of the seventh month the Lord's Feast of Tabernacles begins..."
> —Leviticus 23:24,27-28,34 NIV; read also Leviticus 23b-25

In God's calendar there are three major "appointed times": Passover (a cluster of three feasts), Pentecost, and then the climax of the yearly cycle is the celebration of His Glory at the Feast of Tabernacles. This feast is also a cluster of three feasts.

The seventh month begins with the Feast of Trumpets. It is called *Rosh Hashanah*, the "Head of the Year." It is also known as the "Birthday of the World," or the "Anniversary of Creation." It is a call to awaken! It is a prophetic picture of the rapture of the church, when the "trump of God" sounds, at the second coming.

The ten days after Trumpets are called the "Days of Awe." They are also called days of *"Teshuvah"* which means repentance. It is a time to praise Him and read His Word! It is a time to ask God to reveal any sin in our lives and draw close to God.

The Day of Atonement follows which is a time for our fellowship with God to be restored through repentance. Hebrews 12:1b (NIV) is a perfect description of this day, "*to throw off... the sin that so easily entangles, and let us run with perseverance the race marked out for us.*" It is a time to put all our sins under the Blood of the Lamb and be fully restored to God.

The Israelites were instructed to go out into the countryside and cut down leafy branches and poplars and build tabernacles, or temporary shelters. *Sukkot* is the Hebrew name for this feast. It was to remind them that God had them live in tabernacles when He brought them out of Egypt. They were to feast for an entire week and rejoice before the LORD. This is also a prophetic picture of our living forever in heaven with Jesus.

PRAYER

> *Lord, in Your Word on the last day of the Feast of Tabernacles You said: "If anyone is thirsty, let him come to me and drink" (John 7:37). Lord, we want this living water! We want Your Holy Spirit! Come Jesus come and fill us with Your Holy Spirit!! In Your name. Amen.*

Leviticus

DAY 64

THE YEAR OF JUBILEE

> And you shall consecrate the fiftieth year, and proclaim liberty throughout all the land to all its inhabitants. It shall be a Jubilee for you; and each of you shall return to his possession, and each of you shall return to his family.
> —LEVITICUS 25:10; READ ALSO LEVITICUS 25-27

THE WONDERFUL LIBERTY of a Jubilee was joyfully announced through all the land. It was proclaimed on the tenth day of the seventh month on the great Day of Atonement and was announced with the sounding of the trumpet. When the trumpet sounded, it meant more than the land receiving an extra year of rest. Land was to return to the family it was originally given to, and people (including slaves) were expected to return home.

This meant that no family would be forever without land. Every fifty years, every family would have the opportunity to start again.

> Debts were to be remitted, slaves emancipated, and so the mountains of wealth and the valleys of poverty were to be somewhat levelled, and the nation carried back to its original framework of a simple agricultural community of small owners, each sitting under his own vine and fig-tree.[48]

This very verse of scripture about the Year of Jubilee is on our Liberty Bell in Philadelphia, Pennsylvania. This Liberty Bell rang on the day of America's birth, and it was a prophetic picture of Christ, our Jubilee, who forgave our debts and freed us from spiritual slavery.[49] This is the heritage of America!

It is also our inheritance as believers. One day each of us shall return to our possession. Believers are citizens of heaven (Philippians 3:20). The day will come when we will hear the blast of a trumpet (1 Thessalonians 4:16-17) and come to our true and eternal home.

PRAYER

> *Father in heaven, we are so thankful for this promise of Jubilee for every believer, and every family! What was stolen will be returned, what was lost will be found, what was broken will be restored! Amen!*

NUMBERS

DAY 65

THE PRIESTS AND LEVITES

> Take a census of the whole community of Israel by their clans and families. List the names of all the men twenty years old or older who are able to go to war. You and Aaron are to direct the project, assisted by one family leader from each tribe.
> —Numbers 1:2 NLT; read also Numbers 1-3

As Numbers begins, the nation of Israel was camped at the foot of Mount Sinai. The people had received God's laws and were preparing to move out to receive their land. A census was taken to determine the number of men fit for military service. The book is named for this census, or numbering of the people.

The nation of Israel was organized according to tribes for several reasons. First, because it was an effective way to manage and govern a large group. Second, because it made dividing the Promised Land easier. The tribes were placed in specific places around the Tabernacle, which was in the center of the camp.

The Levites were set apart to care for the Tabernacle and minister to the people. All the priests were of the tribe of Levi, but not all the Levites were priests. Only Aaron and his descendants were appointed to the priesthood.

The Kohathites, Gershonites and Merarites were families of Levites who were assigned special tasks in Israel's worship. Moses and Aaron were of the family of the Kohathites because they were the sons of Amram, the son of Kohath, the son of Levi. They were to care for the holy things of the sanctuary.

There is a tremendous contrast between the priesthood of Aaron in the Old Testament and the priesthood of Christ in the New Testament. Aaron and his sons were the only ones who could carry out the duties of the priests and approach God. Now that Christ in our High Priest, anyone who follows him is also called a priest. Now all Christians can come boldly into His presence without fear (Hebrews 4:14-16).

PRAYER

> *Father in heaven, we are so thankful that You have made us kings and priests to serve You. We are so thankful that we can come boldly to the throne of grace to obtain mercy and find grace to help in time of need! (Hebrews 4:16). In Jesus' Name. Amen.*

Numbers

DAY 66

THE BLESSING

> The Lord bless you and keep you; The Lord make His face shine upon you, and be gracious to you; The Lord lift up His countenance upon you, and give you peace."
> —NUMBERS 6:24-26; READ ALSO NUMBERS 4-6

THIS BLESSING WAS one way of asking for God's divine favor to rest upon others. This blessing helps us understand what a blessing was supposed to do. There are five parts here of asking God to:

1. Bless and protect you. This shows the love of God. He loves to bless His people. He blessed Adam and Eve at the beginning in Genesis 1:27. Jesus blessed the people as He left them in Luke 24:51: *"Now it came to pass, while He blessed them, that He was parted from them and carried up into heaven."*

2. Make His face to shine upon you. To have the glorious, happy face of God shining upon man is the greatest gift anyone could have. He is pleased, not because of who we are or what we have done, but because we are in Jesus Christ.

3. Be gracious to you: The idea is that God shows tender mercy and care for His people.

4. Lift up His countenance upon you. This means to pay attention to you and show you favor. In his book, *"Living in the F.O.G. (Favor Of God),"* Mike Evans shares four principles that are life changing. They are: Radical Forgiveness, Radical Obedience, Radical Generosity, and Radical Humility.[50]

5. Give you peace. Peace here means "nothing missing, nothing broken." Peace in Hebrew means "a sharp, threshing instrument to destroy chaos and confusion."

PRAYER

Father in heaven, You wanted so much to give Your blessing, and have a powerful blessing pronounced upon Your people, that You dictated this exact blessing to Aaron to pronounce upon the people. Lord, we receive this blessing today. Lord, we speak this blessing over ourselves, and over all who cross our paths today. May we walk in the favor of God today with radical forgiveness, obedience, generosity, and humility. Amen and Amen!

DAY 67

GUIDANCE FOR THE JOURNEY

> Now on the day that the tabernacle was raised up, the cloud covered the tabernacle, the tent of the Testimony; from evening until morning it was above the tabernacle like the appearance of fire.
> —NUMBERS 9:15; READ ALSO NUMBERS 7-9

A PILLAR OF CLOUD by day and a pillar of fire by night guided and protected the Israelites as they travelled across the wilderness. This was not a natural phenomenon—it was very supernatural. In a sense, Jesus is the cloud by day, and the pillar of fire at night!!

This was more than proof of God's presence. The cloud by day and the fire by night were actual helps and comforts to Israel. The fire at night was obviously a comfort to Israel in the midst of a dark wilderness, and the cloud by day would be a shade from the hot wilderness sun.

We can see this in Psalm 121:5, *"The LORD is your keeper; the LORD is your shade at your right hand. The sun shall not strike you by day, nor the moon by night..."*

Israel needed to be guided by God each step of the way to make it to the Promised Land. When the cloud moved, they moved. When the cloud stayed, they stayed. They only went where the presence of God led them, and they only stayed where the presence of God stayed.

Believers today must, in the same way, be led by the presence of God. When Paul says, *"let the peace of God rule in your hearts"* (Colossians 3:15), he means the presence of God's peace is to be an umpire or a judge in our hearts.[51]

In the Lord's presence is peace, wisdom, and joy. Psalm 16:11 says: *"You will show me the path of life; In Your presence is fullness of joy; At Your right hand are pleasures forevermore."*

PRAYER

> *Father in heaven, we praise You that You sent the cloud by day and the fire by night to guide, direct and protect Your people. This is a wonderful type of Your Son, Jesus, who is the fire by night. He gives light in the darkness. He gives fire so we can burn brightly for Him! He is also the cloud by day that covers us and leads and guides us!! Jesus, be the Light and Cloud Covering in my life today! In Your Name. Amen.*

DAY 68

TIME TO MOVE

> Rise up, O Lord! Let Your enemies be scattered.
> And let those who hate You flee before You.
> —NUMBERS 10:35b; READ ALSO NUMBERS 10-11

IT HAD BEEN two years since Israel left Egypt. Having received God's travel instructions through Moses, the Israelites set out from Mount Sinai toward the Promised Land.

How do you organize over one million people to march forward? The LORD spoke to Moses to make two silver trumpets. When they blew both of them, all the congregation was to gather. When they blew only one, just the leaders were to gather. Short staccato blasts were used in battle and to order the camps to move off in a specific order.[52]

Also, they were to be sounded in the day of gladness. God will use the sound of a trumpet to gather His people for the ultimate assembling together-the rapture of the church, to meet the Lord in the air (1 Thessalonians 4:16-18).

As they departed from the mountain of the LORD on a journey of three days, the ark of the covenant of the LORD went before them. Whenever the ark set out, Moses said:

"Rise up, O LORD! Let Your enemies be scattered, and let those who hate You flee before You." And when it rested, he said: *"Return O LORD, to the many thousands of Israel"* (Leviticus 10:35-36).

Moses was saying to the LORD to go ahead of them to protect them. This is a very fitting prayer for every believer to pray! This is also a fitting prayer to remember the glory and strength of our resurrected Lord!! When Jesus rose up, were not all His enemies scattered? Who dared oppose Him? Is not our victory found in His risen glory? We can pray this prayer by ourselves and lay hold upon the horns of the altar.

PRAYER

> *Father, we come to You in Jesus' Name and ask that our enemies be scattered and those who hate You to flee before us! Thank You so much that You go before us and make a way for us through uncharted territories. When we are troubled on all sides by our enemies, You make a way where there seems to be no way!!! We give You thanks and glory!! In Jesus' Name. Amen.*

DAY 69

COMPLAINING CONTINUES

> And all the children of Israel complained against Moses and Aaron...and said to them, "If only we had died in the land of Egypt! Or if only we had died in this wilderness!'"
> —NUMBERS 14:2; READ ALSO NUMBERS 14-15

THE ISRAELITES WERE so filled with unbelief that they wanted to select a leader to go back to Egypt! Moses and Aaron fell on their faces to intercede that the Lord would pardon their iniquity.

Joshua and Caleb spoke to the congregation and reminded the people that the promised land was exceedingly good. They reasoned with the people to not rebel against the Lord, but that the Lord would surely protect them.

Because of their unbelief, rebellion, and complaining, the LORD said that the carcasses of those who had complained would fall in the wilderness, except for Joshua and Caleb. They had spied out the land for forty days; the result of their disobedience was that they would be in the wilderness forty years. Their children would be the ones that would go in to take the promised land-- the ones they had said would be victims.

The Israelites then further disobeyed and decided that they would go in and take the promised land. Moses said that it was not going to work, and that they would be defeated. And they were.

Many times, we are tempted to be discouraged and quit.

One example of a person who had the spirit of Joshua and Caleb was Winston Churchill. During World War II he said, "... *never give in, never give in, never, never, never, never in nothing great or small, large or petty, never give in except to convictions of honor and good sense. Never yield to force, never yield to the apparently overwhelming might of the enemy.*"[53]

What can we learn from their mistakes?

PRAYER

> *Father, we can learn a great lesson from the Israelites. Unbelief, rebellion, and complaining end in defeat and failure. Help us not to faint in our minds but to have the perseverance of mind that says, "I will never give in. I will never quit. I can do all things through Christ who strengthens me. Jesus always leads me in a triumphal procession." In His Name. Amen.*

Numbers

DAY 70

HONORING GOD'S CHOICE

> What right do you have to act as though you are greater than anyone else among all these people of the LORD?
> —NUMBERS 16:3B NLT; READ ALSO NUMBERS 16

KORAH, WHO WAS a first cousin of Moses, was not satisfied with serving with the other Levites of the family of Kohath. He also wanted the priesthood. He accused Moses of pride and exclusionary leadership. He had a following of 250 people.

Moses was horrified and threw himself down with his face to the ground. He told them that tomorrow they were to come with their incense burners and incense and the LORD would show whom He had chosen to be priest.

They came the next day with their incense burners. Moses told everyone to get away from the tents of Korah, Dathan and Abiram. Moses warned that if the ground opened up and swallowed them alive, it would show they had despised the LORD. This is exactly what happened. The 250 bronze incense burners were hammered into a sheet of metal to cover the altar.

The next day the whole community was muttering, and Aaron had to run out into the people with his incense burner to stop the plague. 14,700 people were killed.

Aaron's work as high priest here is a picture of our high priest Jesus and His work on our behalf. We were guilty sinners deserving judgment. Jesus was unjustly accused and attacked. He prayed on our behalf and ran to save us. He stood between death and life for us.

Korah's story gives us many warnings: (1) Don't let desire for what someone else has make you discontent with what you already have. (2) Don't try to raise your own self-esteem by attacking someone else's. (3) Don't expect to find satisfaction in power and position: God may want to work through you in the position you are now in.[54]

PRAYER

> *Father in heaven, help us to show honor and appreciation for those You have placed over us!! Help us to give thanks for our calling and not compare ourselves to others. In Jesus' Name. Amen.*

Numbers

DAY 71

THE BUDDING OF AARON'S ROD

> And it shall be that the rod of the man whom I choose will blossom; thus I will rid Myself of the complaints of the children of Israel, which they make against you.
> —NUMBERS 17:5; READ ALSO NUMBERS 17-18

THE LORD INSTRUCTED Moses to take twelve wooden staffs, one from each tribe of Israel, and write each tribal leader's name on his staff. Aaron's name was to go on the staff of the tribe of Levi.

These staffs were to be placed in the Tabernacle in front of the Ark of the Covenant. God said that the rod belonging to the man that He had chosen as priest would have buds sprout on it.

A rod was a symbol of authority, because shepherds would use a rod to guide and correct the sheep. *"Thy rod and thy staff shall comfort me"* (Psalm 23:4b). The rod of Moses became a serpent, turned the waters into blood, and brought forth plagues. Jesus, in His divine authority is given the title "the Rod" (Isaiah 11:1), as He is the Rod from the stem of Jesse.

God said the rod of the man He chose would blossom. What a miraculous sign—the blossoming of dead wood! Fruitfulness is present when godly authority and leadership are being practiced.

The day after Moses placed the rods before the LORD in the tabernacle, behold, Aaron's rod had sprouted and put forth buds, had produced blossoms and even yielded almonds!! God clearly showed His choice of Aaron as priest. In Hebrews 7, Jesus is declared our high priest of the order of Melchizedek, not Aaron.

Aaron's rod was placed in the Ark of the Covenant as yet another sign of Israel's sin: the tablets they broke, the manna they complained about, and Aaron's rod meant to answer their rebellion and show His choice. This is the place the high priest placed the covering blood of sacrifice over these reminders of Israel's sin.[55] The blood made atonement for their sin, as Jesus' blood makes atonement for our sin.

PRAYER

> *Father, we are amazed at the miraculous signs you gave your people of Your choice of those in leadership. We accept that Jesus is forever chosen as Your High Priest after the order of Melchizedek. Amen!!*

DAY 72

THE WATER OF PURIFICATION

> Eleazar the priest must then take cedarwood, a hyssop branch, and scarlet thread and throw them into the fire where the heifer is burning.
> —NUMBERS 19:6 NLT; READ ALSO NUMBERS 19

THE PROVISION FOR purification is a type and shadow of Jesus Christ. The people of Israel were to bring a red heifer that had no physical defects. The color red would resemble blood; this is a type of Jesus' blood. The heifer was to be without any blemish, which is a type of Jesus' sinless nature.

The red heifer was to be slaughtered outside the camp. Jesus was crucified outside the city walls of Jerusalem. Some blood was sprinkled seven times toward the front of the Tabernacle. As High Priest, Jesus' blood was put on the altar for our cleansing.

Then the heifer was burned. Eleazar the priest then took cedarwood, a hyssop branch, and scarlet thread and threw them into the fire where the heifer was burning.

Each of these three items has a special significance.[56] Cedar is extremely resistant to disease and rot and is well known for its quality. Some think the cross Jesus was crucified on was made of cedar.

Hyssop was not only used with the cleansing ceremony for lepers, but also Jesus was offered drink from a hyssop branch. David said in Psalm 51:7, *"purge me with hyssop."*

Scarlet, the color of blood, pictures the cleansing blood

of Jesus on the cross. Scarlet was used in the veil and curtains of the tabernacle (Exodus 26:31). It was also the sign of Rahab's salvation (Joshua 2:21). It was also the mocking "king's robe" put on Jesus at His torture by the soldiers (Matthew 27:28).

PRAYER

> *Father in heaven, we pray along with the psalmist David, "Purge me with hyssop and I shall be clean; Wash me, and I shall be whiter than snow....Create in me a clean heart, O God, and renew a right spirit within me. Cast me not away from thy presence, and take not thy Holy Spirit from me. Restore unto me the joy of thy salvation, and uphold me by thy free Spirit" (Psalm 51-10-11 KJV). In Jesus' Name. Amen.*

Numbers

DAY 73

MOSES' BIG MISTAKE

> Take the rod; you and your brother Aaron gather the congregation together. Speak to the rock before their eyes, and it will yield its water; thus you shall bring water for them out of the rock, and give drink to the congregation and their animals.
> —NUMBERS 20:8; READ ALSO NUMBERS 20

THE CHILDREN OF Israel came to Kadesh where Miriam died, and there was no water there. They complained miserably with no faith in the God who split the Red Sea for them to walk through.

The LORD spoke to Moses to "Speak to the rock" and it would bring forth water. However, Moses was so angry that he struck the rock *twice*. God had told him to take the rod, but he was not to use it as he did at Mount Sinai (Exodus 17:6). The rod was a symbol of his authority from God.

Then Moses lectured the nation with an attitude of anger and contempt for the people of God. Then he magnified himself by saying, "Must we bring water for you out of this rock?" It was as if he and God divided the work fifty-fifty. Is there pride here?

Not only did he strike it, but he struck it twice out of anger and frustration. Still, the water did come out, so he was for the time being, justified. And God shows His mercy for the people.

However, the rock was a beautiful picture of Jesus'

redemptive work (1 Corinthians 10:4). Jesus, being struck once, provided life for all would drink of Him. But it was unnecessary and unrighteous that he would be struck twice, because the Son of God needed only to suffer once (Hebrews 10:10-12).[57]

Since he did that, Moses was not allowed into the promised land. Another person would be chosen to lead the people into the promised land. (However, on the Mount of Transfiguration, we see Elijah and Moses with Jesus, so he made it in after all!)

PRAYER

> *We thank you Jesus, that You are our Rock, our fortress, our high tower. You are our strength, in whom we trust. We thank you for this beautiful picture of You, and that even though Moses failed in complete obedience, You still had mercy, and provided for the needs of the people. As the Psalmist David said, "For who is God, except the LORD? And who is a Rock except our God?" (Psalm 18:31). Amen.*

Numbers

DAY 74

THE BRONZE SERPENT

> Then the Lord said to Moses, "Make a fiery serpent, and set it on a pole; and it shall be that everyone who is bitten, when he looks at it, shall live."
> —Numbers 21:8; READ ALSO Numbers 21

True to form, as Israel journeyed around the land of Edom, the soul of the people became very discouraged on the way. And guess what? They complained. This time they not only complained against Moses like their fathers did, but they complained against God and Moses. They were about to pass into the Promised Land, and now they were acting in unbelief.

The Lord sent fiery serpents and many of the people died. Something needed to happen, or they would never enter the Promised Land. The people came to Moses and repented for speaking against the Lord and against him. Moses prayed for the people.

The Lord told Moses to make a fiery serpent and set it on a pole, and everyone who was bitten and looked at the pole, would live.

Jesus referred to this very event in John 3:14-15: *"And as Moses lifted up the serpent in the wilderness, even so must the Son of Man be lifted up, that whoever believes in Him should not perish but have eternal life."*

But you may ask, "How can a serpent have a similarity to Jesus?" The Bible says that Jesus became sin for us, that we might become the righteousness of God in Christ. A bronze serpent on a pole speaks of sin that has been judged.

The people were saved when they *looked* at the serpent. In the same way, we are saved when we look to Jesus. Isaiah 45:22 says: *"Look to Me and be saved, All you ends of the earth!"*

PRAYER

> *Thank You Jesus, that You became sin for us. You became that snake on the pole when You took our sin. It is only looking to You that we are saved from our sin. Thank You for the cross, Lord! Thank You for the price You paid. Bearing all our sin and shame, in love You came, and gave amazing grace.[58] In Jesus' Name. Amen.*

DAY 75

BALAAM, THE DONKEY, AND THE ANGEL

> Then the Lord opened Balaam's eyes, and he saw the Angel of the Lord standing in the way with His drawn sword in His hand; and he bowed his head and fell flat on his face.
> —Numbers 22:31; read also Numbers 22

AFTER THE ISRAELITES had victory over Sihon and Og, they traveled to the plains of Moab. Balak, the Moabite king, was terrified and sent a message to Balaam the prophet to come and curse Israel.

God told Balaam that he was not to curse them, for He had blessed them. God told him to not go with these Moabites.

God ended up letting Balaam go with these people, but He was angry about his greedy attitude. Balaam claimed he would not go with them, but his resolve was beginning to slip. The wealth he was being offered blinded him, so he could not see how God was trying to stop him. The desire for money can also blind us from hearing God's voice and doing His will.

God allowed Balaam to go with the men. However, His anger was aroused and the Angel of the Lord took His stand in the way. The donkey saw the Angel of the Lord standing in the way with His drawn sword in His hand and went out of the way into the field. Balaam beat the donkey to turn her back onto the road.

Then the angel of the LORD stood between two vineyard walls. When the donkey saw the Angel of the LORD, it tried to squeeze by and crushed Balaam's foot. Balaam beat it again.

Then the LORD opened the mouth of the donkey and miraculously gave the donkey the ability to speak, and she rebuked the prophet for his ungodly punishment of her.

When the LORD opened Balaam's eyes, and he saw the Angel of the LORD standing in the way with His drawn sword in His hand; he bowed his head and fell flat on his face. The LORD said that Balaam's way was perverse before Him. Since the Angel of the LORD told Balaam that his sin was against Him personally, it indicates this is an Old Testament appearance of the Son of God.[59]

PRAYER

> *Help us Lord to not be like the horse or like the mule, which have no understanding (Psalm 32:9). We yield our hearts to You. In Jesus' Name. Amen!*

DAY 76

BALAAM GIVES MESSIANIC PROPHECY

> A star will rise from Jacob; a scepter will emerge from Israel.
> —Numbers 24:17a nlt; read also Numbers 23-25

Time and time again, Balak, king of Moab, tries to get Balaam to curse Israel. However, every time he tried to curse Israel, he ended up blessing them. In Chapter 23:8 (NLT) he prophesied: *"But how can I curse those whom God has not cursed? How can I condemn those whom the LORD has not condemned?"*

Then again in chapter 23, Balaam delivered this prophecy in verses 19-20 (NLT): *"God is not a man, that he should lie. He is not a human, that he should change his mind. Has He ever spoken and failed to act? Has He ever promised and not carried it through?"* He then said that God had blessed, and he could not reverse it!

By now, Balaam saw that God intended to bless Israel, so he did not resort to divination. In Balaam's final prophecy he said, *"A star will rise from Jacob; a scepter will emerge from Israel."*

The star out of Jacob is often thought to refer to the coming Messiah. It was probably this prophecy that convinced the astrologers to travel to Israel to search for the baby Jesus. It may seem strange that God would use a sorcerer like Balaam to foretell the coming of the Messiah. But this teaches us that God can use anything or anyone to accomplish his plans.[60] This does not mean that God condones sorcery; in fact the Bible condemns it (Exodus 22:18; Revelation 18:23).

Balaam could not curse Israel, but later in chapter 31 we see that Balaam had the idea of teaching Balak to put a stumbling block before Israel, by getting them to eat things sacrificed to idols, and to commit sexual immorality (Revelation 2:14). This led to one man bringing a Midianite woman into the camp right before Moses. Phinehas, son of Eleazar followed them into their tent and killed both of them, but not before 24,000 had died because of the plague (Numbers 25:6-9).

PRAYER

> *Our Father in heaven, we ask that the Daystar would arise in our hearts and bring healing to our hearts, families, and nation. In Jesus' Name. Amen!*

DAY 77

INHERITANCE FOR DAUGHTERS

> Why should the name of our father be removed from among his family because he had no son? Give us a possession among our father's brothers.
> —NUMBERS 27:4; READ ALSO NUMBERS 26-28

THIS PORTION OF scripture deals with five daughters of Zelophehad. He had no son, and normally the land inheritance should be passed from a father to his sons in Israel, not to the daughters. The daughters came to Moses and asked what would happen to their father's inheritance. Would it be assumed by someone else? Would his name live on with his inheritance?

Moses went to the Lord and asked Him about it. Even though the son-in-law provided a dowry, that was not the same as land inheritance.

The Lord said that the daughters of Zelophehad spoke what was right, and that they should surely be given a possession of inheritance among their father's brothers, and that the father's inheritance should indeed pass to them.

God seemed pleased that the daughters of Zelophehad had brought this issue to Moses. He then declared that the inheritance should go to the daughters.

The problem this created, though, was that if they married out of their tribe, the land would go with them. They were later told to marry only within their tribe.

The remarkable thing is that the daughters were women of faith. They were concerned about dividing up what they did not yet have in their hands but knew they would possess by faith. This is the Bible's first instance of an appeal for equal rights for women. They were a wonderful example of appealing to God and trusting in Him to see that they were not denied. They were concerned about injustice. They also displayed a godly spirit in complying with the elders' decision that they should marry within their tribe. God defended them when they allowed Him to be their Deliverer/Provider.

PRAYER

> *Lord, thank You for honoring the request of these women of faith. Thank You that You are a God of justice and mercy to all!! Amen.*

DAY 78

OFFERINGS FOR THE FEAST OF TRUMPETS

> And in the seventh month, on the first day of the month, you shall have a holy convocation. You shall do no customary work. For you it is a day of blowing the trumpets.
> —NUMBERS 29:1; READ ALSO NUMBERS 29-31

THE LORD SPOKE to Moses to command the children of Israel to bring offerings to Him. They were to offer burnt offerings, grain offerings, sin offerings, and drink offerings. These offerings were to be given at the daily offerings, Sabbath offerings, monthly offerings, and offerings at all the feasts.

At the Feast of Trumpets, they were to offer a burnt offering as a sweet aroma to the LORD: one young bull, one ram, and seven lambs in their first year, without blemish (Numbers 29:1-6).

This burnt offering was a consecration offering. The Israelites were saying to God, "I am consecrating myself and my substance to You. In offering Himself on the Cross, Jesus consecrated Himself to God to do His will, and to become the sacrifice for our sins. Romans 12:1 says: *"I beseech you therefore, brethren by the mercies of God, that you present your bodies a living sacrifice, holy, acceptable to God, which is your reasonable service."*

The grain or meal offering had to do with the Israelites giving of their substance and God prospering them. This serves as a type of abundant life that Jesus' death, burial and resurrection made available to all born-again believers. The flour was a type of the perfect humanity of Christ. Oil is a picture of the Holy Spirit.[61]

The sin offering represents forgiveness for the sins we commit against God. One of the first declarations that was made about Jesus was that *"you shall call his name JESUS, for He will save His people from their sins"* (Matthew 1:21).

The drink offering represents His blood. Jesus at the Last Supper said to *"drink from it, all of you"* (Matthew 26:28).

PRAYER

> *Lord, we rejoice in seeing You in every detail of Your sacrifice. We thank You for the cross!! In Jesus' Name. Amen.*

DAY 79

CITIES OF REFUGE

> You must give the Levites six cities of refuge, where a person who has accidentally killed someone can flee for safety.
> —NUMBERS 35:6A NLT; READ ALSO NUMBERS 32-36

CITIES OF REFUGE were designated for people to flee to if they had killed someone accidentally. These cities were for the protection of Israelites, resident foreigners, and traveling merchants, from dead person's relatives who wanted to avenge the death.

There were three cities set aside east of the Jordan, and three cities on the west in the land of Canaan. The slayer could not be killed before being tried by the community.

If the murder was premeditated, the slayer would be punished with death by the victim's nearest relative. However, if the hostility was not premeditated, or was accidental, the slayer could run to the city of refuge. He had to stay there until the death of the high priest. If he ever left the city of refuge before the death of the high priest, he was no longer safe. After the death of the high priest, he could return to his own property.

All murderers must be executed, but only if there was more than one witness. No one could be put to death on the testimony of only one witness. Likewise, no ransom payment could be accepted for the slayer, so he could return early to his property. This ensured that the land would not be polluted, for murder pollutes the land.

Jesus is our city of refuge. *"God is our refuge and strength, a very present help in trouble"* (Psalm 46:1). "Both Jesus and the cities of refuge are open to all, not just the Israelite; no one needs to fear that they would be turned away from their place of refuge in their time of need."[62] Jesus will never turn anyone away!!

Both Jesus and the cities of refuge are the only alternative for the one in need; without this protection, they will be destroyed.

PRAYER

> *Lord, we rejoice in You that You alone are our city of refuge!! Your ears are always open to us. Your arms are always open to us to comfort us. Your eyes are always open to our needs. Your heart is always touched by the feelings of our infirmities. You never leave us!!! In Jesus' Name. Amen.*

DEUTERONOMY

DAY 80

WHAT GOD HAS DONE

> I am giving all this land to you! Go in and occupy it, for it is the land the Lord swore to give to your ancestors, Abraham, Isaac, and Jacob, and to all their descendants.
> —Deuteronomy 1:8 NLT; read also Deuteronomy 1-2

In the book of Deuteronomy, Moses calls Israel to remember who God is and what He has done. Since they lacked faith, the old generation had wandered for 40 years and died in the wilderness. They left Egypt behind, but they never entered the Promised Land.

While they were on the east bank of the Jordan River, Moses began to recount their history. He told how he selected wise and respected men as their leaders. He instructed the judges to be perfectly fair, to not only Israelites, but also to the foreigners. He said they must never favor the rich, but they must be fair to the lowly and great alike.

Then he recounted how when they arrived at Kadesh-Barnea, he allowed them to send out scouts into the Promised Land. They chose twelve spies. However, ten came back with a bad report. Only Joshua and Caleb said they were well able to take the Promised Land. However, because of the bad report, Israel rebelled against the command of God and refused to go in. They forgot that He said that He would go in ahead of them and fight for them! Even after He had led them through the wilderness and gave them the cloud by day and the fire by night (Exodus 13:21-22), led them through the Red Sea, gave them bread from heaven and water from the rock, they did not trust Him to protect them and give them victory. As a result of this, they wandered in the wilderness forty years, until that whole generation had died.

After this, God gave them victory over Sihon of Heshbon and Og of Bashan. They took possession of their land.

PRAYER

> *Lord, help us always to rehearse our victories, and remember all that You have done!! Help us not to look at the giants and the seemingly unsurmountable odds, and just trust You instead! Help us not to be disobedient like Israel was but help us to keep our eyes on You and not on the circumstances!! In Jesus' Name. Amen.*

DAY 81
THE GREATEST COMMANDMENT

> Hear, O Israel: The Lord our God, the Lord is one! You shall love the Lord your God with all your heart, with all your soul, and with all your strength. And these words which I command you today shall be in your heart. You shall teach them diligently to your children, and shall talk of them when you sit in your house, when you walk by the way, when you lie down, and when you rise up.
> —Deuteronomy 6:4-7 read also Deuteronomy 4-6

This passage provides the central theme of Deuteronomy. In Hebrew these verses are known as the *Shema*. It describes who God is and what our duty is towards Him.

The LORD our God, the LORD is one! (v. 4). God is one God and not many. Other religions worship many gods. We worship one God, existing in three persons.

We are to love the Lord with all our heart, and all our soul, and all our mind. Jesus called this the first and great commandment. What God wants most from us is our love. Jesus said the second was like it: *"You shall love your neighbor as yourself"* (Matthew 22:39). This fulfills the whole law.

This great command must first be in our heart, and then it must be communicated to our children. We are to teach these words to them when *"you sit in your house, when you lie down, and when you rise up"* (v. 7). Teaching God's Word is not to be relegated to the church or Christian school. Parents need to love, live and teach God's Word to their children themselves.

In Jesus' day, Jewish people wore phylacteries on their forehead or hand, held there by leather straps containing this passage. Jesus condemned abuse of the wearing of phylacteries as some would make them large as a display of greater spirituality. In the end times, there will be a Satanic imitation of this practice when the number of the Antichrist will be applied to either the hand or forehead of all who will take it (Revelation 13:16).

PRAYER

> *Lord, help us always to love You with all our heart, our soul, and our mind. Help us to do a good job of teaching Your Word and Your ways to our children, that they too will love and obey You!! Amen!!*

DAY 82
A CHOSEN PEOPLE

> For you are a holy people to the Lord your God; the Lord your God has chosen you to be a people for Himself, a special treasure above all the peoples on the face of the earth.
> —DEUTERONOMY 7:6 READ ALSO DEUTERONOMY 7-9

THE ABOVE PASSAGE clearly tells that Israel is a chosen people. They are a special treasure to the Lord. The first and foremost reason, is that it was through the Israelites that Jesus, our Messiah was born.

Paul said of the Israelites: *"...to whom pertain the adoption, the glory, the covenants, the giving of the law, the service of God, and the promises; of whom are the fathers and from whom, according to the flesh, Christ came, who is over all, the eternally blessed God"* (Romans 9:4-5).

The covenants Paul spoke of were the Old and New Covenants. The Old Covenant was the 10 Commandments. The New Covenant was the Covenant of His blood, which was shed for our salvation and healing.

These are some of the promises Paul referred to in Romans 9, spoken of in Deuteronomy 7-8:

- *You shall be blessed above all peoples; there shall not be a male or female barren among you or among your livestock* (Deuteronomy 7:14).

- *And the LORD will take away from you all sickness, and will afflict you with none of the terrible diseases of Egypt which you have known, but will lay them on all those who hate you* (Deuteronomy 7:15).

- *And you shall remember the LORD your God, for it is He who gives you power to get wealth that He may establish His covenant which He swore to your fathers, as it is this day* (Deuteronomy 8:18).

PRAYER

Lord, help us always to love and honor the Israelites through whom came our Messiah. Thank You that Your promises to them are also for us now. We pray for the peace of Jerusalem. We pray that all of Israel will recognize Jesus as their Messiah! In His Name. Amen.

Deuteronomy

DAY 83
FEAR THE LORD

> You shall fear the Lord your God; you shall serve Him, and to Him you shall hold fast, and take oaths in His name. He is your praise, and He is your God, who has done for you these great and awesome things which your eyes have seen.
> —Deuteronomy 10:20-21 read also Deuteronomy 10-12

The Hebrew word for "fear" here is *yare*, which means to not only be afraid, but also to revere, to have in reverence. Reverence is a word meaning to respect with awe and affection.

When we love the Lord, we will want to serve Him and give Him praise for all the great and awesome things He does on our behalf.

Love and obedience go hand in hand. In Deuteronomy 11:22-12:6, we read that *"if you carefully keep all these commandments which I command you to do—to love the LORD your God, to walk in all His ways and to hold fast to Him,"* He will:

- Drive out the nations greater than yourselves.
- Every place on which your foot shall tread will be given to you, from the River Euphrates to the Western Sea.
- No man will be able to stand against you.

- Give you a choice: the blessing if you obey the commandments of the LORD, and the curse if you do not obey the commandments of the LORD.

- Lead you to cross over the Jordan and go in to possess the land which the LORD your God is giving you, and you will possess it and dwell in it.

- Prepare a place for the LORD your God (tabernacle) where you will offer your burnt offerings. (All the sacrificial system was a type and shadow of Jesus).

PRAYER

Lord of heaven and earth!! We praise and thank You for all the blessings you bestow on us as we love and obey You. May we understand that fearing You is really loving you and even being infatuated with You. In Jesus' Name. Amen.

DAY 84

GENEROSITY TO THE POOR

> If there is among you a poor man of your brethren, within any of the gates in your land which the Lord your God is giving you, you shall not harden your heart nor shut your hand from your poor brother, but you shall open your hand wide to him and willingly lend him sufficient for his need, whatever he needs.
> —DEUTERONOMY 15:7-8 READ ALSO DEUTERONOMY 13-15

THIS REMINDS US of Galatians 6:10 – *"Therefore, as we have opportunity, let us do good to all, especially to those who are of the household of faith."* Our charitable giving is to begin with those brothers and sisters closest to us, though it certainly can extend outward from there.

These verses show the compassion of God for the poor, downtrodden, and the slaves. The Lord commanded the Israelites to cancel debts the seventh year, and to free their Hebrew slaves. These people had to sell themselves into slavery because of their debt. This made certain that a "bankruptcy" did not harm an Israelite all their life. This would give the slave, about to be freed, hope and greater incentive to please his master.

In Deuteronomy 15:16-18, we see that if a slave did not want to go away from them because he loved them and their house, then the master should take an awl and thrust it through his ear to the door, and he would be the master's servant forever.

Jesus is the great fulfillment of this willing slave. Jesus

said prophetically in Psalm 40:6: *"My ears You have opened"*...This speaks of the "opening" of the ear in the bond-slave ceremony. Jesus was the willing bond-slave of God the Father. Also, Isaiah 50:5-7 shows that Jesus' character as the willing slave was most perfectly shown in His sufferings at the cross: *"The Lord GOD has opened My ear; and I was not rebellious, nor did I turn away."*[63]

PRAYER

> *Dear Father in heaven, help us to be a willing slave of God. Even as Paul stated in Galatians 6:17: "From now on, let no one trouble me, for I bear in my body the marks of the Lord Jesus." Help us, like Paul, to be a slave for life to Jesus. Help us to realize that nothing we own is really ours, but it is a gift on loan to us to accomplish Your work on earth. In Your name we pray. Amen.*

DAY 85
THE PROPHET

The Lord your God will raise up for you a Prophet like me from your midst, from your brethren. Him you shall hear.
—DEUTERONOMY 18:15 READ ALSO DEUTERONOMY 16-18

VERSE 15: *"THE LORD your God will raise up for you a Prophet like me."* Moses was saying that the LORD would raise up a prophet that would be like him.

"From your midst, from your brethren." This not only meant that He would be an Israelite, but that He would be a "man of the people" – He would be one of them.

"Him you shall hear": Like Moses this Prophet would command the attention of the nation. This means that Israel should listen to this Prophet, and that they would listen to this Prophet.[64]

"According to all you desired of the LORD your God in Horeb": (verse 16). Like Moses, this Prophet would be a mediator, representing God to the people, and representing the people before God.

"(I) will put My words in His mouth, and He shall speak to them all that I command Him": (verse 18). Like Moses, this Prophet would speak God's Word.

"I will require it of him." (verse 19b). In other words, there will be a great penalty for rejecting this word. Acts 3:23 says, *"And it shall be that every soul who will not hear that Prophet shall be utterly destroyed from among the people."*

Some thought that John the Baptist might be this

Prophet (John 1:19-21). *"And they asked him, 'What then? Are you Elijah?' He said, 'I am not.' 'Are you the Prophet?' And he answered, 'No.'"* The New Testament plainly tells us that Jesus is this Prophet (Acts 3:19-26, Acts 7:37).

PRAYER

> *Dear Father in heaven, it is so exciting to read in Your Word, that You sent your Son to be the Prophet spoken of in Deuteronomy 18, written about 1400 B.C. How wonderful that from the beginning of time you had a Redeemer, a Savior, a Prophet of Prophets, planned to bring salvation and healing to Your children! We praise and bless Your Name! In Jesus' Name. Amen.*

Deuteronomy

DAY 86

AN EYE FOR AN EYE

> One witness shall not rise against a man concerning any iniquity or any sin that he commits; by the mouth of two or three witnesses the matter shall be established.
> —Deuteronomy 19:15 read also Deuteronomy 19-21

ONE WITNESS WAS never enough to establish a fact in a Biblical court of law. Two or three witnesses were needed to establish a matter.

This is not only because it is possible for one witness to lie without having his story confirmed. It is also because one witness can be confused or mistaken in his testimony. It cannot be just "my word against theirs."

If the judges, after diligent inquiry discern that the witness is a false witness, then they would do to him as he thought to have done to his brother. This was the way to put evil from among them.

Verse 21 says: *"Your eye shall not pity: life shall be for life, eye for eye, tooth for tooth, hand for hand, foot for foot."* This law was meant to be a check for revenge, not a license for revenge.

Jesus quoted this passage in Matthew 5:38-39. He does not say that the eye for eye principle is wrong: He just condemns the use of it to get revenge against someone who has personally offended us. He did not reject it as a principle of justice which should operate in the courts of the land. He said it was wrong in interpersonal relationships. For private relationships He wanted a reaction of good in the face of evil. His was a law of loving our enemies and doing good to those who hate us and praying for those who persecute us (Matthew 5:44).[65]

PRAYER

> *Our Father in heaven, help us in discerning motives of our hearts. Help us to walk in righteousness and justice. Help us also to walk in love for our brothers. Help us to see our brothers through Your eyes, and while not ignoring what is wrong, remembering to pray and forgive those who would testify wrongly against us. If we are in the wrong, help us to ask forgiveness. Help us always to speak the truth in love. In Jesus' Name. Amen.*

DAY 87
LAWS CONCERNING DIVORCE

> When a man takes a wife and marries her, and it happens that she finds no favor in his eyes because he has found some uncleanness in her, and he writes her a certificate of divorce, puts it in her hand, and sends her out of his house, ...
> —Deuteronomy 24:1; read also Deuteronomy 22-24

According to these laws, divorce was allowed in Israel, but it was carefully regulated. It was only allowed when there was a certificate of divorce.

The Hebrew word translated divorce has as its root the idea of "a hewing off, a cutting apart" – it is the amputation of that which is one flesh.[66]

The grounds of divorce included finding uncleanness in the wife. The Pharisees came to Jesus and asked Him, *"Is it lawful for a man to divorce his wife for just any reason?"* (Matthew 19:3). So Jesus talked to them about what marriage was really about. He said that from the beginning, God made them male and female, and that when they are married, they become one flesh. Therefore, what God had joined together, no one should separate.

He continued by saying that Moses permitted them to divorce because of the hardness of their hearts, but this was never God's will from the beginning.

Paul went on to say this about marriage in Ephesians 5:25-27:

> *Husbands, love your wives, just as Christ also loved the church and gave Himself for her, that He might sanctify and cleanse her with the washing of water by the word, that He might present her to Himself a glorious church, not having spot or wrinkle or any such thing but that she should be holy and without blemish.*

Jesus was saying that a relationship between husband and wife is like the relationship that Christ has with the church.

PRAYER

> *Lord, help us to have soft hearts of love for our spouse. Take out the stony parts of our hearts. Forgive us for selfishness. Help us to love each other like Christ loves the church!! In Jesus' Name. Amen.*

DAY 88

BLESSINGS ON OBEDIENCE

> Now it shall come to pass, if you diligently obey the voice of the Lord your God, to observe carefully all His commandments which I command you today, that the Lord your God will set you high above all nations of the earth. And all these blessings shall come upon you and overtake you because you obey the voice of the Lord your God.
> —Deuteronomy 28:1-2; read also Deuteronomy 25-28

Notice carefully the word "if." The covenant God made with Israel contained three main things: the law, the sacrifice (that was part of the law), and the choice.

> The idea behind the choice is that God was determined to reveal Himself to the world through Israel. He would do this either by making them so blessed that the world would know only God could have blessed them so; or by making them so cursed that only God could have cursed them and cause them to still survive. The choice was up to Israel.[67]

Here are some of the blessings: (verses 3-13)

- Blessed shall you be in the city and in the country.
- Blessed shall be the fruit of your body...
- Blessed shall you be when you come in or when you go out.

- You will lend to many nations, but you shall not borrow.
- The Lord will make you the head and not the tail.
- You shall be above only and not be beneath.

An obedient Israel would be blessed everywhere. The Lord wanted to establish them as a holy people to himself. He wanted a special relationship with them.

The opposite would be true if they were disobedient. Instead of the blessings, they would receive the curses.

PRAYER

> *Lord, help up to choose obedience and be recipients of all the wonderful blessings that come with that choice. Help us to choose to follow in Jesus' footsteps who was obedient to God. In Jesus' Name. Amen.*

Deuteronomy

DAY 89

CHOOSE LIFE

> I call heaven and earth as witnesses today against you, that I have set before you life and death, blessing and cursing; therefore choose life, that both you and your descendants may live.
> —Deuteronomy 30:19; read also Deuteronomy 29-31

Under the terms of the Old Covenant, Israel had a choice: life or death, good or evil. It was up to them. God would glorify Himself through Israel one way or another.

If Israel would be obedient, they would see blessing. If they were disobedient, then they would perish. It was based on their conduct.

It is important that we do not relate to God on the terms of the Old Covenant; we have a better covenant. Under the New Covenant, our relationship with God is not based on what we do for God, but on what Jesus has done on our behalf.

The Israelites were charged to choose life. We today are also confronted with a choice. But our choice does not focus on "Will I obey God or not?" but on "Will I trust in Jesus for my standing before God?"

Jesus is still asking the question, *"Who do you say that I am?"* (Matthew 16:15), and our choice in answering that question determines our eternal destiny.

After Moses challenged them to choose life, he went on in verse 20 to say, *"that you may love the Lord your God, that you may obey His voice, and that you may cling to Him, for He is your life and the length of your days; that you may dwell in the land which the LORD swore to your fathers, to Abraham, Isaac, and Jacob, to give them."*

It is important to note that when we choose life, both we and our children will live (verse 19). The Bible says in Deuteronomy 30:6, that the LORD will circumcise our hearts <u>and</u> the hearts of our descendants, to love the LORD with all our heart and soul that we may live. This is God's promise to us for our children!

PRAYER

> *Dear Father, we choose life today that both we and our children will live!!!! In Jesus' Name. Amen.*

Deuteronomy

DAY 90
MOSES LIKE JESUS

> There has never been another prophet like Moses, whom the Lord knew face to face. The Lord sent Moses to perform all the miraculous signs and wonders in the land of Egypt against Pharoah, all his servants, and his entire land. And it was through Moses that the Lord demonstrated his mighty power and terrifying acts in the sight of all Israel.
> —Deuteronomy 34:10-12 nlt; read also Deuteronomy 32-34

Several things made Moses like Jesus:

- The Lord knew him face to face. He had remarkable personal intimacy with God. Jesus knew His Father and only did what He saw His Father do.

- Moses was unique in the number and kind of miraculous works in which he was associated. Jesus healed the sick, raised the dead, cleansed the leper, and cast out demons.

- Moses was unique in the power and authority with which he led the nation of Israel. Jesus said in Matthew 28:18, *"All authority has been given to Me in heaven and on earth."*

- In Moses all the great offices of Israel were seen: prophet, ruler, judge and priest. In Jesus we see Prophet, Priest, and King of

Kings and Lord of Lords. Philippians 2:10-11 states, *"that at the name of Jesus every knee should bow, of those in heaven, and of those on earth, and of those under the earth, and that every tongue should confess that Jesus Christ is Lord, to the glory of God the Father."*

- Before Moses died, he spoke a blessing over the tribes of the children of Israel. For example:

- *"Let Reuben live and not die, nor let his men be few"* (Deuteronomy 33:6).

- As Jesus was about to ascend to heaven, *"He lifted up His hands and blessed them. Now it came to pass, while He blessed them, that He was parted from them and carried up into heaven"* (Luke 24:50-51).

PRAYER

Dear Father, we also choose to be like Jesus. "To be like Jesus, to be like Jesus, all I ask, to be like Him. All through life's journey from earth to glory. All I ask to be like Him!" Amen.

NOTES

1. Cindy Jacobs, "The Sabbath's Rest," G.I. News (Colorado Springs, Colorado: Generals of Intercession, 1995), Vol. 4, No. 1, January/February, 1.

2. Dr. Richard G. Lee, ed., The American Patriot's Bible, (Nashville, Tennessee: Thomas Nelson, Inc., 2009), 6.

3. David Guzik, enduringword.com.

4. Ibid.

5. Ibid.

6. Benny Hinn, The Blood, (Lake Mary, FL: Creation House, 1993), 38-39.

7. Joyce Wells Booze and Cathy Ketcher, editors, Sacrifice & Triumph, (Springfield, MO: Assemblies of God World Missions, 2003), 73-79.

8. Enduringword.com (Morgan)

9. Enduringword.com (C.S. Lewis)

10. David Guzik, enduringword.com

11. Dr. Richard G. Lee, ed., The American Patriot's Bible, (Nashville, Tennessee: Thomas Nelson, Inc., 2009). 578.

12. Paraphrased from Dutch Sheets, Giants Will Fall: Become A History Maker, (Colorado Springs, CO: Dutch Sheets Ministries, 2018), 56.

13. www.ap.gilderlehrman.org

14. Lee, The American Patriot's Bible, 586.
15. Ibid., 1334.
16. Ed Silvoso, Prayer Evangelism, (Ventura, CA: Regal Books, 2000), 39-40.
17. Paraphrased from Copeland, Believer's Voice of Victory, December —Volume 48: No. 12 (Fort Worth, TX: Kenneth Copeland Ministries, 2020), 5-6.
18. Brian Simmons, The Book of Genesis, The Passion Translation, (United States of America, BroadStreet, 2019), 70.
19. David Guzik, enduringword.com
20. Simmons, The Book of Genesis, The Passion Translation, 83.
21. David Guzik, enduringword.com
22. Simmons, The Book of Genesis, The Passion Translation, 87.
23. David Guzik, enduringword.com
24. Simmons, The Book of Genesis, The Passion Translation, 104.
25. E-sword, (F.B. Meyer).
26. Simmons, The Book of Genesis, The Passion Translation, 129.
27. Ibid., 134.
28. Enduringword.com (Cole)

29. Jack Hayford, ed. New Spirit-filled Life Bible, (Kingdom Dynamics) (Nashville, TN: Tomas Nelson Publishers, 2002), 79-80.

30. David Guzik, enduringword.com

31. Mary Nell Wyatt, Battle for the Firstborn, (Springhill, TN: Royal Hill Press, 2020), 148.

32. David Guzik, enduringword.com

33. Enduringword.com, (Meyer).

34. Robert Heidler, The Messianic Church Arising, Denton, TX, (Glory of Zion International Ministries, 2006), 168-169.

35. Wyatt, The Battle for The Firstborn, 156.

36. Paraphrased from Battle for The Firstborn, 17.

37. Ibid., 232.

38. Paraphrased from Elijah House School of Ministry, Training Course 201: Level 1 Prayer Ministry, (Coeur d'Alene, ID: Elijah House, Inc., 2011) 109-110.

39. Enduringword.com (Kaiser)

40. John Matthews, The Covenant in Jesus' Blood, (Coon Rapids, MN: Scarlet Thread Ministries, 2013), 124.

41. Alice Smith, Beyond the Veil, (Ventura, CA: Renew Books, 1997), 91.

42. Paraphrased from Stanley Howard Frodsham, Smith Wigglesworth, Apostle of Faith, (Springfield, MO, Gospel Publishing House, 1974), 82.

43. Paraphrased from James W. Goll, The Lost Art of Intercession, (Shippensburg, PA, Destiny Image, 2007), 24.
44. David Guzik, enduringword.com
45. www.newhoperevivalchurch.com/azusa-street-revival-william-seymour
46. Ibid.
47. Enduringword.com (Harrison).
48. Enduringword.com, (Maclaren).
49. Paraphrased from Giants Will Fall: Become A History Maker And Take Out The Giants, Colorado Springs, CO: Dutch Sheets Ministries, 2018), 52.
50. Mike Evans, Living in the F.O.G. (Favor Of God), Phoenix, AZ: TimeWorthy Books, 2012), 10.
51. David Guzik, enduringword.com
52. Enduringword.com (Wenham)
53. www.dutchsheets.org GH 15, March 4, 2021
54. Ronald A. Beers, ed., Life Application Study Bible, (Wheaton, IL: Tyndale House Publishers, 1996), 225.
55. David Guzik, enduringword.com
56. Ibid.
57. Ibid.
58. Darlene Zschech, https://www.youtube.com/watch?v=FCPP-qovLtI
59. David Guzik, enduringword.com
60. LT

Notes

61. Marilyn Hickey, The Tabernacle Syllabus, (Denver, Co" Marilyn Hickey Ministries, 1998), 183-188.
62. David Guzik, enduringword.com
63. David Guzik, enduringword.com
64. David Guzik, enduringword.com
65. Enduringword.com (Thompson).
66. David Guzik, enduringword.com
67. Enduringword.com (Harrison).

www.ingramcontent.com/pod-product-compliance
Lightning Source LLC
Chambersburg PA
CBHW072004070526
44583CB00015B/1334